DANCING MY JOURNEY

Nikki Stein

Copyright © 2024 (Nikki Stein)
All rights reserved worldwide.

No part of the book may be copied or changed in any format, sold, or used in a way other than what is outlined in this book, under any circumstances, without the prior written permission of the publisher.

Publisher: Inspiring Publishers,
P.O. Box 159, Calwell, ACT Australia 2905
Email: publishaspg@gmail.com
http://www.inspiringpublishers.com

 A catalogue record for this book is available from the National Library of Australia

National Library of Australia The Prepublication Data Service

Author: Nikki Stein
Title: Dancing My Journey
Genre: Non-fiction

Paperback ISBN: 978-1-923087-43-9
ePub2 ISBN: 978-1-923087-42-2

After undergoing recent heartache from an abortion, the author, a mum-of-four and small business owner finds herself revisiting key moments of her eventful life journey leading up to this pivotal point. Her journey is one dotted with unexpected turns and challenges, but also underpinned by joy from her passion for dance, travel around Australia, and love for her family.

CONTENTS

Author's foreword vii
1. The Start 1
2. Evans Head 9
3. The Trip and Social Suicide! 16
4. High School and First Love 22
5. The Move to the Big Smoke: Sydney 32
6. The Visit! 41
7. Hit the Road Again 46
8. Marriage or Bust 52
9. Andrew and the Ones that Got Away! 56
10. Tristan 65
11. Leo the Baby Born in the Bush 73
12. Marly, my Marvellous Mistake 85
13. Antonio Lost 92
14. Reaching and Shooting Stars 99
15. Fire, Flames and Fleeing 102
16. Here We Are 107
17. The Trouble with Tom 111
18. The Delay of my New Chapter 115
19. The Truth? 121
20. The Gap Year 124
21. Here I Begin 129

Acknowledgements 135

AUTHOR'S FOREWORD

So here I am, starting that book… It's been an ongoing joke among my friends that my life should be written down. My life has been and is always a drama. Nothing comes easy, nothing is straightforward and I can't think of a time when all was calm. On my coffee dates with my friends, I feel I should supply them with popcorn and, at times, tissues. I don't even mean to be dramatic or cause such heightened emotional reactions. I'm just telling them about my day or the week leading up to that day. Of course, at times, past years get brought up too, and as I talk about my experiences on whatever the topic is, it's often a story of obstacles, battles or something I lived through to tell the tale.

Even writing this now, I cringe. Am I just a drama queen? Do I attract drama and a lot of bad luck? Am I whinger? I often look back on certain moments and think, shit, who would want to be my friend? Do I actually offer anything of value to any of my friends? And I hope they don't think of me as the needy friend that is so over the top in all aspects of her life. I'm exhausted thinking about my life and the day-to-day motions of it. Is it too much to expect my friends and family to live through it with me? I'm kind of going off-track here, but I didn't know how to begin this intro, so it's sort of turned into ramblings. Anyway, to sum up those ramblings, I guess I just wanted to express my concern for my fantastic group of friends that keep me sane in my insane life. My parents too – my dad and my mum (step mum) – they are my sounding board in life. They keep me on keeping. So much love! Aww.

So why did I decide to start this book? Well, just another heartache and so another chapter to add, so start now! Today I found out I was pregnant. This should not be such an awful thing … but this would be my 5th child and probably about my 8th pregnancy. I just can't have another baby, with the past year being hell, my youngest being 16 months. My family is full and my husband is not of sound mind. So today, I made a decision even though so heartbreaking, that I will not be having this baby. It makes me hate myself, hate my husband for not being able to get out in time, grrr, and for not getting a vasectomy last year. My mental state hasn't always been straight A's either, and parenting alone with my four children has been challenging. Yes, I have my husband, and yes, we are still together, but he has been rather absent in the fathering role a lot. Anyway, I will go deeper into that ISSUE later. Chapter something-a-rather!

So, me making the decision not to have this baby has added a lot more guilt, and feelings of confusion. I'm going to get rid of this one — when only 10 years ago I couldn't conceive and had multiple miscarriages. It was all those years ago that I broke really and never gained myself back in one piece. This is all a timing thing and a way for me to learn some kind of life lesson. I think I'm done with the lessons now, life, so stop being so shit. As you can see, I'm a bit bitter. I hope that by writing this out, it will be a therapy of some sorts. Don't get me wrong, I know a lot of people have more shit than me and I'm not in a competition. I'm just writing out as best as I can remember the events of my life. I owe it to my kids and family, and to entertain my friends!

I'm going to start at the start, I guess...

CHAPTER 1

The Start

Of course, I don't remember the very beginning of my life, only what I have seen in photos. Some bits pieced together by my Nan. I was born in Griffith, in southern NSW in 1979. Yep, so almost 40. Perhaps this is my mid-life crisis outlet. Anyway, my parents were young and lived at my grandparents' farm at the time. My mum was only 19 when she married my dad and he was only 20, I think. They pretty much had me a year later. Mum (Diana) was a stunningly beautiful woman, she was a model, but I believe she was sick. Mentally I think she was very sick, and when my dad met her, my Nan jokes about him being so blinded by her beauty that he overlooked all her paranoia, spitefulness, violence and moodiness. It was not long after I was born that she hit her peak and was admitted a few times. She was diagnosed with schizophrenia. Being the early 80s, she was heavily sedated, then released with meds to be taken ongoing. Dad would find her meds down the sink and, as we now know, schizophrenia is progressive, so with her not medicating, she got worse. We moved around a lot and ended up in North Queensland. Dad was always trying to keep her happy and did what she wanted.

We moved into a derelict property in the Tablelands in Mount Molloy. I remember a big house on stilts, surrounded by bush, a little creek down the back. We had no power, no hot water. I was sure that we were squatting in that house, but Dad reckons we were renting. My brother Leon arrived four years after me while we were squatting in that house. Dad was working as a bricklayer and worked hard. My sister Summa arrived about eighteen months after Leon. By then, I was attending the local primary school and have strong clear memories around this time.

Diana was really unwell and often said very confusing things to me ... as a child some things you just shouldn't know about. The conversations she used to have with me lead me to now believe that Diana was sexually abused as child and that she grew up in a very violent home within a caravan park. Dad later in life explained to me how Diana had told him about her father doing things to her and her sister, and it was the reason she never let her father next to her in adult life. He was never allowed to come to the house. She often accused my dad of the same thing that was done to her and she had a real paranoia about it. I remember her asking all the time about it ... have I been touched and punishing me for walking around naked (I was four). Also telling me not to hug Dad, and not to sit on his lap etc. I was scared to go near Dad at that time. I didn't even talk to him for about a year. Diana would abuse me when dad was at work. She would hit me with things. Her favourite was a kite stick – it fucking stung. It would leave welts, and I will always remember that whip sound it made as it came through the air towards me. I eventually hid it down the back of the old fire oven.

She would say disgusting things to me. I can't really remember what now, but I remember always being petrified of her. She locked me outside, not dressed in the middle of winter. Again, I don't remember why but she was pissed off and told me to get out (I was sitting at the table eating breakfast before school). She locked the door behind me and I was outside all day. She had a sleep and I was sitting with the puppies in the dirt outside her window. I remember they were big swinging stained-glass windows. She swung them open, looked at me and asked, "What the hell are you doing out there?" There was so much confusion and a sense of hatred towards me. And so many more incidents but I have worked hard on leaving this part of my life in the past and have had to deal with this aspect of my childhood ever since.

Dad was given a super hard time all the time, and Diana often went missing. She used to take us kids and run to women's shelters claiming Dad was being abusive. Dad would spend weeks looking for us before eventually finding us. He became really good friends with the Sergeant of the Mount Molloy police. I don't know his name but he always helped Dad track us down.

Diana got involved with the Jehovah's Witnesses and this worsened her state. I remember I got the lead in the Christmas play at school (Mary). Diana marched up to the school demanding that I was not to be involved in the play, going on about religion ... I was devastated. I remember my teacher comforted me. The next day for the play, I was supposed to go sit in the library and not even watch. My teacher came and got me from the library. She had made me a fantastic costume. I couldn't be Mary, but what's more important than Mary (besides Jesus)? THE STAR. The teacher had made me a star costume and she told me to just stand on the stage on a chair and twinkle away. I so twinkled. I was so happy, and I remember this teacher forever because of it. I never told Diana, and it's possible the teacher told me not to.

I was never really allowed to have friends. My first ever friend was Jemima, we were besties. I was lucky in the sense that her mum and dad were complete hippies and didn't care much about what other people thought. I'm pretty sure Jemima's mum knew what was going on in my house and how Diana was with me. I spent a lot of time at Jemima's and remember it was her mum that made sure I did. She would always come and pick me up and drop me home and I know she had heated conversations with Diana, which I'm pretty certain were about me. I loved staying at Jemima's. I was free ... free to play, dress up, be silly. It was probably my happy place. Jemima got to talk to her mum like a real person. They were best friends and always so happy ... I was happy to know her and her family. I kept in contact with Jemima even after I moved away and got to visit and stay with her once more when I was a teen back visiting the area.

Diana tried really hard to stop my friendship with Jemima, banning me from seeing her, calling us little lesbians and stuff (I think we practised kissing like grown-ups once and she saw us). If it hadn't been for Jem's mum who wouldn't take no for an answer, I probably wouldn't have seen her anymore and my childhood would have not had any fond memories, not to mention play and socialisation.

Mount Molloy is a tiny town at the foot of the Atherton Tablelands. It literally has one street. Surrounded by mountains, from Cairns, it was a steep climb up and over the mountain range to get to Mount Molloy. It was about 50 minutes of winding and rainforest-bordered road to get there. I remember always getting car sick on that road. Mount Molloy had a small primary school, a pub, a post office, a bakery, a corner shop and that was about it, really. So, isolation was definitely a factor in our lives then— there were no playgroups or ways for people to get together unless it was at the pub. Diana didn't have any friends. I know she joined the tennis club in Mount Molloy, but it didn't last long. I feel as though isolation may have played havoc on her mental health and the fact that we were so hidden away socially meant many of her issues and behaviours went unnoticed for a long time.

There were a few people around that time in my life that had an impact upon me and gave me a bit of joy and a feeling of a childhood at times. Dad's best friends, Rick and Cheryl, had no kids of their own and Cheryl loved nothing more than to look after me, and later my brother Leon and sister Summa. They lived by the beach at Newell Beach in North Queensland. I think Dad and Rick worked together bricklaying, otherwise Rick was a fisherman, badly. Their house was no more than a beach shack and was full of all things sea life and how to catch it. Cheryl worked at the local pub as a barmaid. I think I went to Rick and Cheryl's when Dad wanted to visit them or he had to work and I needed sitting. Cheryl was the kindest, most loving and kooky lady. Her warmth made me happy and I loved visiting them. We saw a lot more of them when Diana went through a phase of needing to be out of Mount Molloy and made Dad move us to Mossman. We had a few moves around that area. I remember living in a yellow house surrounded by cane fields, with cane toads everywhere. We also lived in a flat that sat under a massive water tank. A flat on the trainline in the centre of Mossman.

I can't remember how old I was then, and I can't remember which siblings were around then either. Anyway, we didn't stay for long, and went back to Mount Molloy.

Diana was getting worse and running away with us kids every second week. We got on a plane once and went to see her aunty in Townsville. I remember Diana being very sick at the time, and I believe she was committed while we were in Townsville. I went to stay with some cousins. I had no idea who they were, but I remember the cousins were all older. Diana had my youngest brother then too, Tom. He was born rather unwell and this was supposedly due to the meds Diana had been given. The Aunt contacted Dad and he came and got us from Townsville. I can't remember if this was the first time or second time that he had done this. Anyway, Diana came home at some stage and we resumed life.

Diana burned all of Dad's record collection and all my baby things, pretty dresses that Nan had bought me and other random items were burned too. Dad couldn't believe it when he got home and we were sitting by the fire pit watching everything burn. Why? They were evil, his records were by demons, and my baby things were also evil. Not long after the burn-off, Mum tried to burn and blow up our car. It broke down a lot she was angry at it, I guess. She threw things at Dad a lot, and often locked him out the house. She threw an old antique sewing machine at him once from the top of the stairs. I don't know how he got away unharmed ... he walked in the door at the base of the stairs and she was at the top of the 15-something stairs and pushed the machine at him, ranting about something as it crashed its way to the bottom.

I was often helping her do crazy stuff. I like to think I didn't know any better. I definitely remember trying to always stay on her good side and trying to get approval from her. I do know, even though I was only four or five years old, I had a constant feeling of fear and sadness, and I knew she didn't like me. I don't remember her ever telling me she loved me or that I was important to her. I still wonder even today why she didn't love me. Had I burdened her life? Had me coming along ruined the attention of others for her? My belief now though, seeing and living with mental illness, is that it's selfish. Schizophrenia is a very selfish disease and makes you think only of yourself. Love and compassion are hard to process for those with it, and I think this was the case for Diana. Her sickness gave her a strong jealousy and paranoia. She always thought people were out to get her or saying bad things about her and when I came along as a new baby, I got attention. In her sick mind, I was out to take away her shine and somehow detract from her beauty. Possibly she had post-partum depression that went undetected too.

Her dislike towards me was confirmed to me when she started to leave me behind when she would run. She dropped me to school one day and didn't come back to get me. I went to the principal's house, which was next door to the school. Dad didn't even know I was there. He assumed she had taken me with her. The principal eventually called the Sergeant who was able to get in contact with Dad and let him know where I was, and he came and got me very late that night. We went home to the empty house and, for the first time ever, I properly spoke to Dad and told him about home life, how it is when he isn't there, and what happens while he is at work. I told him the things Diana says to me and how I feel sad most of the time. That night, I sat on my dad's lap and talked to him. I think it made him happy — not happy by what he was hearing, but happy because he finally understood why I was scared of him and wouldn't speak to him with her around.

While Diana had disappeared this time around, I had to go and stay with some friends of Dad's. I remember it was a family of four kids, a mum, and Dad's friend. He was a harsh man, very strict and looking back now, probably cruel. His kids were scared of him. I remember not being allowed to talk above a whisper. His kids hated him. I knew to stay out of his way, stick to the rules and not talk much, which wasn't hard for me because it was a lot like home.

I'm not certain how long I stayed there for. I remember going away on holidays with the mum and their kids. I was there until Dad had sorted out the finding of Diana and my siblings. I remember Dad taking me home eventually. Diana was home. I was happy to see her and ran to hug her. She looked me up and down and said,

"What's with the dress?" The family I had been staying with had been great second-hand store shoppers. When I had gone to stay there, I had taken hardly anything with me, so the mum had taken me on one of their hunts and I had got a few things. One of them was a pretty yellow dress with puffy sleeves. What kind of five-year-old girl doesn't love a pretty dress?

Things are a little blurry timeline-wise here ... I know and remember the last time Diana took off. She took all us kids that time and we went only fairly locally to an old lady's house who was a Jehovah's Witness too. I remember us all rocking up to her house and sitting in her little old lady kitchen out the back of the house and eating Iced VoVos. Diana was looking for somewhere to stay and it looked like this was where it was going to be this time. I can't remember how long we stayed but I remember the old lady's kids eventually talking to Diana and asking us to leave.

We went out to the Kombi van we had arrived in and Diana started putting all my siblings in. I got in the front seat and put my seatbelt on. It was then that I saw Dad approaching the car ... he started talking to Diana which escalated into a yelling fight. She locked us all in the car and continued the fight with Dad. She then jumped in the driver's side, with Dad trying to stop her from closing the door. She closed it, locked it and began winding up the window. Dad ran around the van trying to open the doors. He came to my side and I tried to pull up the lock to let him in. Diana reached over pushed it back down. Dad was banging on the window at this stage, Diana was yelling and trying to start the Kombi ... it often didn't start the first few goes. My siblings were crying in the back and I was calling for Dad too. I wanted out so bad. I was scared and didn't want to be with my mum anymore. Dad banging on my window told me to wind the window down. So, I started to ... it was hard and took all my strength to do just a little crack. Diana, I think, had got the Kombi going by this point. Dad got his hands in the window crack and pushed it down halfway. "Take your seat belt off!" he yelled. I reached over and unclipped just in time as Dad pulled my arms up and out of the Kombi and all the way out of the window. Diana raced off in the Kombi with my brothers and sister.

I'm not a hundred per cent sure what happened exactly after that, but I believe Diana and my siblings were found not long after that ordeal. I think that was the end of all of that then. I know Diana cried abuse so Dad couldn't get my brothers and sister. Diana was again committed and my brother Leon and sister Summa were put into foster care. My dad had visitation rights, but he was not able to get them home. While this was going on I moved from a few different friends' homes and even had a week at Jemima's. Until Dad could work out what to do.

It was at this time Dad called on Nan and Pop to help him get the kids. They were soon up in North Queensland and within a few months, Nan and Pop had my siblings in their care. I was then able to join them in NSW along with Dad a couple of weeks later.

CHAPTER 2

Evans Head

I want to talk about my grandparents here. My Dad's parents, Nan and Pop G. — the most beautiful people ever. Nan was a bit of a hard-arse and very proper and particular. However, my moral compass definitely came from them. I work hard and try to do well because of them. My Pop always worked hard and did so much for everyone he loved. He was a gentle, beautiful man who loved my Nan so much, he had created a stable and fruitful life for the love of his life. He treated her like a princess and they did everything together. I only heard them fight over the beans not being cooked long enough or the fact Nan was getting in the way when he was trying to clean up the kitchen after dinner.

Pop died in 2013 and left a massive void in all our lives. He had battled with blood cancer for about 18 months. Just after his 90th birthday he was able to get a window of wellness, enough to travel to his favourite place to holiday in Weipa. My Dad and his brother and sister all went up there, along with Nan, of course. Pop was able to fish his favourite spots on the river, and see the friends he had made up there. He was there a week when he passed away, surrounded by his family in the place he loved most in the world. I was able to talk to him on the phone in his last hour. So much sadness as I write this. Let's go back.

When Nan and Pop took my siblings, we all moved to Evans Head in New South Wales. Nan and Pop had a massive white mansion that sat on the headland of North Evans. My Pop was a builder and had built that house. I couldn't believe how beautiful the house was. I often imagined I was a princess living in a castle on top of that big hill. We were so happy there. Dad soon joined us in New South Wales and we all lived with Nan and Pop. We were well fed, clean, loved and got to have some nice things and toys. I had my first ever birthday party while living there. I went to the local primary school and things seemed calm and normal, I think.

I remember a little disruption from time to time when Diana would try to visit. She even turned up at my school one day. I remember being scared and not wanting to talk to her. She just walked straight onto the playground and found me. The principal came and asked her to leave as she wasn't allowed to see me without supervision and the school was aware of this order. I had been to child psychologists and had DOCS visit a few times. Diana had supervised visitation rights with my brothers and sister, but I didn't have to see her ever again if I didn't want to. That's what I had been told, and I was happy about this. I recall going to court and I guess making a statement about who I wanted to live with and who was I happy around most. I do remember wondering, though, when my siblings went off to visit her, why she never asked to see me. It was all most confusing for my 6-year-old brain, I think.

During our time at Evans Head, life was normal. Us kids all got vaccinated, we had birthday parties, had friends, the tooth fairy visited. We had magnificent bubble baths, ate dessert after dinner, had new clothes and pretty shoes. Dad took my siblings for their visits with Diana and I stayed away.

Dad started dating not too long into our year at Evans. I used to get picked up some afternoons from school by the Mitch family. Dan Mitch was a young boy in my class and his mum, Sally, knew my Nan and had a pick-up schedule for me. Some afternoons I would go back to their house and hang out. There was Emma and a little toddler Brett ... We all became quite close. It was through Sally that Dad met Carrie, Sally's sister who had just gone through a divorce, and had a two-year-old, Dylan. Sally and my Aunty (Dad's sister) were best friends and thought they would send Dad and Carrie on a blind date. They did and, basically, they were smitten. I think I was seven when they met. I thought Carrie was great, really nice and she had the best clothes, so funky. I also remember she smelt really nice. She used to wear LouLou and to this day I could still pick that smell. She would always leave the smell of LouLou everywhere.

I suppose I should mention my brother Tom and his issues here. When Dad was working through the court thing and the custody etc, Dad's cousin Pearl (who lived in Evans Head) had been looking after Tom. He was still a little baby and had not been well. Pearl's kids were grown and she and her husband Richard had put up their hand to look after Tom, to help my Nan and Pop out, give them one less to look after.

I'm not sure how long we lived in Evans Head for, but I remember going driving out to the countryside, in the hills of Lismore (Dunoon) to see an old farmhouse. Carrie was with us – by this time we had known Carrie a while and her son Dylan was just part of the crew. Anyway, the farmhouse was old and run down. It sat on 25 acres and Dad was excited. He had had enough of living with Nan and Pop and was ready to move to the hills. Dad bought that farm, well, Nan and Pop lent Dad the money for the farm and Carrie moved in with us. We were giving it a go as a blended family. Carrie let us call her Mum and we moved through the motions of being a normal step-family, but that was probably the problem. We were trying to be normal. Carrie had taken on four kids that weren't biologically hers and we all came with a history that I guess had made us, us. She tried hard to keep it together, and this resulted in her being strict and a little bitter, I think. I don't feel I was affected by her ways much. I was happy to not live in fear constantly and new-Mum's strictness was nothing compared to what I was coming from with Diana.

My siblings had a harder time, though. They didn't remember what life was like with Diana so they had nothing to compare it to, I guess. Mum was always wanting quiet. She worked shift work as a nurse, and was a stickler for rules and for manners. It's probably also okay to say she was favoured her own son, which I think is an issue that is present in most step families. My brothers and sister noticed this more than I did, and I think they probably found they were being punished for small things or taking the punishment for Dylan.

Tom came to live with us again quite early on in the Dunoon life. He was often going to stay at Pearl's though, as they missed him terribly. He had a hard time with new-Mum only because he was really full-on. He hadn't had a diagnosis at this stage, but he was hyper a lot, naughty, spiteful, had sleeping issues and hurt Dylan a lot. This was not a happy time at Dunoon, and Tom soon moved back to Pearl's full-time and only came to Dunoon on weekends. He was super spoiled there, got everything he asked for and I remember him coming to Dunoon with his bag full of new everything. We all thought it so unfair that he was living the life of an only child and had all the material possessions he could ever possibly want. My siblings and I had not much really. We only got new things for birthdays and Christmas. Anyway, Tom did have a great home and love and was spoilt to no end, but he didn't have his siblings around all the time, which he thinks is his issue in life today ... but Tom is a whole other issue and if I can talk more about him later, I will. He has caused a lot of hurt and drama in all our lives, so perhaps he needs his own chapter later on.

Dunoon life settled and most of my memories of growing up stem from this time. I went through my primary school years in that house. Dad starting to plant his macadamia trees, us helping plant them and fertilize them. I recall, years later, starting high school and picking up those nuts (the trees take at least seven years to produce nuts), my friends coming over in macca nut season and getting roped into picking them up. We got paid with a dinner at McDonald's. My brothers and sister were close in age and I guess this made them close also. My sister was fiery and could fight my brothers and hurt them easily. She could ride motorbikes and loved dirt. She had a great imagination and was/is as stubborn as. When I got into high school, I guess I was more interested in my friends and teenage type stuff and I didn't have much to do with my siblings unless I was bossing them around, creating dances for them or full Christmas productions. Yeah, I was pretty bossy, I liked to keep everything clean and Mum taught us early on how to do washing.

I was obsessed with dancing. I wanted to be a dancer and I worked hard (at home) practising moves, creating dances. Mum and Dad couldn't really afford to put me in lessons and in our area at the time, the early 90s, there wasn't anyone around teaching either. My Nan paid for me to go to ballroom lessons I think for a term, but I didn't like the restrictiveness of the style or the fact I had to dance with a boy. I think I was about 10 when I tried that. Before I move into my high school years, I should talk a bit about my primary years. I went to the local public school. When I started there, there were 52 students. It was a pretty little school about five kilometres from our house. I can't say I was a great student back then. I can't remember working hard all the time. I remember in Year 3 my report card said, "Nikki should stop kissing the boys". I got into so much trouble. I wasn't kissing *boys* though, it was only one: Luke. He was a cheeky kid and was often in trouble himself. Luke was a great friend. We went through all our school life together and he even came to my wedding. Our little public school was a great little school, we had such a wonderful community within that school and most of the kids I went through with I could still call friends today. This time in my life was normal, I think. We played sports on weekends, had sleepovers, made wonderful lifelong friends, went on camping holidays, went on school excursions, school discos (which Dad was DJ for), ate HUMBLE Pies from the tuckshop on a Tuesday. Yes, I think I can say life was pretty good here.

I of course got involved in the school dance shows (festivals) and I remember me and two other girls started a dance group where we danced at special assemblies? Only to *Bananarama* songs. I remember how cool our costumes were: bubble skirts, synch belts, baggy tees and tube socks. One blue, one hot pink, one yellow. We thought we were so cool. The two girls I did that group with, Sari and Tammy, went on to keep dancing for years to come also.

Most of us went off to high school together since our primary school fed into the local high school in Lismore. Most of us even went on the same bus together. I had become really close with Jane by this stage. We had been friends in primary school, but she'd had a best friend who was older. When her older friend went off to high school, we had started hanging out more. Jane had been through a lot growing up. Her mum also had divorced her dad and he had taken his own life about when we were eight or nine. Jane fought with her mum and had seen her mum struggle to stay in relationships. Anyway, Jane and I had become best friends and we were hardly ever apart. I think she was trying to escape her home life and I loved the company. Going into high school, I was scared but Jane was not, or she pretended to not be. She had two older brothers and she knew what to do. I remember going to high school being quite awkward, it was a hard fit trying to find friends. Some of the primary school crew dispersed into other groups. Jane and I stuck together but didn't have a solid crew at first.

The high school was known as the Bronx school of the area. A lot of small hippy towns surround Lismore, with people living in the rainforests off-grid and Nimbin was not far from the town. So, it was a different mix of people, students of the free spirit kind, farmer's kids and a large Aboriginal population also. School uniform was optional and getting caught with pot was a common occurrence. The local Indigenous kids that went to the school were forever causing problems, fighting everyone, stealing and gang-related behaviours. I remember a few times when I had looked at someone or spoke to one of the gang kids and got bullied for months after. One time I got punched in the face by one of them. I was collecting the TV for science class, wheeling it down the hall. Some came out of a class, each one walked past me pushing the TV and they each nudged the TV off the stand, trying to make it tip over. I kept catching it to stop it hitting the floor. It got to the last two kids and the male out of them pushed it again. This time I said to him, "Oh my God, fuck off," as I caught the TV again. He laughed and kept walking. However, behind me was his bigger, older female cousin. I didn't even see her.

She came up behind me, pushed me in the back and said, "What did you say, you little white slut?"

"I told him to fuck off," I said rather sheepishly as my heart was racing. I knew this girl was mean as, often fighting on the streets and making people's life hell.

"You can't call him a fucking black cunt," she said back to me, as she was trying to swipe at me.

The TV stand was in between us, so I just put my head down and kept pushing the TV along trying to get the 15 metres to my classroom. "I didn't call him anything, I just told him to fuck off."

"Ahhh, you being a smart bitch, ah?" she sneered.

"Nope." I just kept pushing the TV. That's when she kind of stumbled backwards. She didn't fall but the stumble was so embarrassing to her that it enraged her more. She jumped at me and popped me one on the cheek. It hurt and tears sprung to my eyes but I didn't cry, I just kept pushing.

"You stupid little white slut," she kept saying, "I'm going to get the brothers onto you, you better watch out, they gonna mess you up and you're gonna get what you deserve."

I reached my classroom and as I got inside the door all I could get out to say was, "Yep, you too, you will get what you deserve."

I was scared for months after that incident, always looking out for the brothers. My friends also gave me a hard time, teasing me about the YOU TOO line: "You'll get what you deserve," saying I sounded like an old lady and what kind of threat was that?

They weren't laughing or teasing six months later when we were all seated in a memorial assembly for that girl. She had died of cancer. Now my friends thought I was a witch that had cursed her. So yeah, our high school did not have the best reputation.

CHAPTER 3

The Trip and Social Suicide!

It was about six months into high school, Year 7, that Mum and Dad decided we were going to go travelling around Australia for 12 plus months. They had been saving for a while and had bought an old 24ft caravan, which Dad had gutted and customised to sleep all four of us kids (Tom was not coming). Our schooling had been sorted, and we were all going to do correspondence. I would teach myself, and Mum would teach the other three. So yep, we were leaving for an adventure of a lifetime. I was so worried. I was going into teenagerness and socially this was going to be suicide. How would I survive without Jane, and my favourite show, *90210*. Back then, no mobiles, no net, so it was tough to stay in contact. I believe we left about June 1991, although it may have been '92. Anyway, we hit the road, leaving the farm in the care of Grandma and Bert (Mum's parents). Heading first to North Queensland, taking our time.

This trip was definitely one to remember and I still have strong happy memories of this time with my family. We had so many adventures, a few breakdowns (mechanically), saw many new interesting places, and we even had our car stolen in Perth. We had a three-month stop in Perth to sort that out. We went to school and lived in a granny flat for a bit while Dad decked out a bus to replace the car. We sold the van and continued our trip in our customised bus. We loved it. I do know I missed home, Jane, my own room. Correspondence was difficult to do while travelling, with large boxes of workbooks and science experiments, lead lighting. Music and Japanese were some of the subjects I had to do. I just did the bare minimum, kept up my maths, English and science.

When I went to school in Perth, I found I wasn't behind anyway, so all was okay there. I made a couple of friends in Perth that I went to school with and one in particular, Kylie, who also loved to dance. Soon, we were making up dances after school and on weekends. We decided to create a little dance show and we took it to main street in Perth Mall, busking. It was through the school holidays and we caught the train into the city every day, taking one of my siblings each day (needed a roadie), a button pusher on the CD player. Anyway, we killed it those holidays. We made over 800 dollars and Mum and Dad said I could spend my half on whatever I wanted. I went shopping at the end of those holidays, buying all the things I thought were cool. We got a dance gig out of it too. Peter Andre was hot shit back then, and he was coming to Perth to do a show for a radio station. The radio station had seen us dancing in the mall to one of Andre's songs and they asked us to dance with him when he came to town. My family and I weren't going to be still around then though, we were moving on. However, Mum and Dad put me on a train in Esperance, and I got to come back to stay with Kylie in Perth so I could dance in the show.

I got put back on a train to meet back up with my family and we continued on our trip across the Nullarbor. I will talk a little about some of my favourite places we saw and the memories that are attached to those places. Cape York was great. We did the old telegraph track, so all 4-wheel driving and it took two days to go 60 kilometres. So many river crossings. We broke down on one of the crossings and had to camp by the river for a couple of days until our friends that we were travelling that section with us returned with the required part. I remember sitting on the bank of the river watching the other cars pass through, or get bogged, us kids sitting in the sandy shallows making things out of gum leaves and swimming all day.

The long stretches of beaches in WA were where we would pull up and stay for days. Long mud and sand flats out to crystal blue water where we would all snorkel with Dad around the coral bommies, Dad often spearing crays or fish, and pointing out sharks to us. That's usually when I would freak out and exit the water but my siblings were not scared. At one place we stopped at, we went to go out for a dive. There was an old jetty and we wanted to swim around it. We got into the water and started snorkelling. We were in for no more than 10 minutes when I saw a sea snake bobbing towards us. I grabbed Leon's arm to tell him and he shrieked. We turned to go the opposite way, away from the snake, but there was another and another. By this time, we had signalled to Dad and when Dad saw we were actually surrounded, he thought we should probably exit the water. Dad had to navigate us through the snake water and we were all pretty hysterical by the time we got out of there. When we got to the shore, it was then we saw all the washed-up dead snakes — hundreds and hundreds of them. It had been the winds. The winds had been so hard it was washing them ashore. WA is known for its sea snakes, so I guess we had seen most of them there that day. We didn't go back in the water there, and spent our days playing on the flats, in the rock pools.

Another memory I have of that place (which I think was 80 Mile Beach) was my sister out on the flats when she got called out for something, got up and started running. But we could see something jumping up at her every second step, and as she got closer, you could see things hanging off her. She by this point was about 20 metres away and was screaming. We rushed down to meet her... she had octopuses all over her, she even had one stuck to her face. It was the funniest thing I have ever seen. Dad was trying to pull them off her, she was hysterical. The octopuses live in the rock pools and as Summa was running past them, they just saw her as a flash and thought she was food. We had octopus for dinner that night.

We did a lot of free camping on that trip as money was not abundant. We free camped a lot through the Northern Territory, and got to see some beautiful untouched places. We swam our first time with crocodiles in the Northern Territory. We were heading out to a billabong that was supposed to be an oasis in the desert. There was a historical site out there also that Mum was wanting us to see. Sightseeing was top on Mum and Dad's essential must-dos for the trip, experience being high in the education department/schooling. It had been really hot driving out there. It was a long dirt road and our car, being an old LandCruiser, had no aircon. The old caravan was big and rattly so we were driving slowly. We didn't get to the oasis, which I think was called Palm Springs, until it was dark. We pulled up the van in a clear area by the water. We couldn't see much. The lights from our camp shone on the black water and we could make out pandanus palms hanging over the water. Dad and Mum did the quick set up and started dinner. Me and my siblings grabbed some torches to look around a bit. We were looking out into the water, imagining how great the swimming would be in the morning. Our torches skimmed around the water. We saw red eyes in multiple spots around the water. We called Dad to come and look.

"Oh yes, that's crocs," he said. We gasped. "They are only freshwater ones they will be okay to swim with in the day," he explained.

The next day, it was hot from 7am and we sat under the caravan awning, looking at the still cool water. The place really was an oasis, just a water hole surrounded by palms, rock faces and gum trees. We were too scared to go in the water after the eyes we had seen the night before, so we sat and whinged for hours. It was around 11am that we heard some vehicles coming and then saw the dust cloud along the road on the horizon. A minibus and a convoy of about three troop-carriers pulled up by the billabong. The bus doors opened and a group of Aboriginal children and women got out. All bare feet and loud in chatter, the troop carriers let out a couple more kids and then the carriers, now just full of Aboriginal men, sped off. The children all jumped straight into the water, some waving to us as they jumped in. The women sat under the trees, or some hopped into the water too. They all looked like they were having so much fun. My sister went over to the water's edge and sat. She then started chatting with some of the kids, and next some came over to the van with her. We chatted with them for a bit. They asked lots of questions and wanted to see in our 'rich person van'.

"It's hot, hey, why don't yas go swimming?" one of the older girls said to us.

We said about the crocodile eyes we had seen the night before.

"Aah, freshies okay yeah, they don't bite, they eat fish," she said.

That was all we needed to hear, not that we didn't believe Dad, just a second opinion, I guess. We then spent the rest of the day swimming and exploring with the Koori kids. They even told us their story of the billabong and the shape of the rock face being done by the rainbow serpent in the dreamtime. Just on dark, the men in the troop-carriers returned. They were all piled in the back sitting on top of dead cows. The men had been out hunting for the day. The women got a big fire going and some meat was carved off the animals. We went back to the van to have dinner. An Aboriginal man in an Akubra holding a massive slab of meat knocked on the door. He handed Dad the meat, saying about us joining them around the fire. The meat was for us for later, but to come and share some of the other beasts with them. We did and sat around with them by the fire. This was a great experience for us. We had not had positive experiences with the Indigenous people from home, so to have met the real true Aboriginals of the outback was really special.

From then on, we had no trouble swimming with freshwater crocodiles. It was even in Kakadu at a water hole that I put some goggles on and swam on top of them watching them as they slept on the sandy bottom about 15 feet down.

I was always reading, my head constantly in a book. It annoyed my parents a lot. They thought I was missing out on my surroundings. I didn't really care, I was in full teen mode by now. I had had enough of my little siblings and having to be with them all the time. All I wanted was to meet a cute boy and perhaps have my first kiss. You see, the books I was reading a lot were Mills and Boon. Yep, so bad, but in most towns, the swap or second-hand book places had a lot of Mills and Boon. So, this was the start of my impression of what love, romance and relationships should be like. My parents were very much in love. I saw this relationship as a positive one. But it's not until later in life when you realise what you really want in a partner. My Dad is a great husband and a fantastic father. He has always done all he could to keep Mum happy and has always given her attention, speaks to her every day, often multiple times in a day, makes her tea every morning, gets her up every day for work. Anyway, yeah, they have a top relationship.

Back when I was a teen, I wanted a Mills and Boon love in my life. I think at that time, I resented my parents for taking me away from my life. I don't remember hating being there. I just remember missing people my own age. I got a little reprieve when we were in Perth and I went to school, and also when we stopped for a couple of weeks at Coral Bay not long after that. Coral Bay is a busy tourist destination in WA. Monkey Bay is there also, where you can swim and feed the dolphins. It was in Coral Bay that I got to run around with some of the young teens who were there on holidays from Perth. I remember hanging out in the park down at the beach and even held hands with a boy. I can't remember his name now, but he was cute with a Justin Bieber look to him. He was 15 and I was 14, I think.

We went home to Dunoon 14 months after we had started our trip. We were returning to the farm with an extra. Mum was having a baby. My brother Jimmy was due to be born in November, a couple of months after we got back.

On our return, we had a welcome back party and some of my old friends came. I remember how different everyone looked. They had all grown and all had had trouble with social acceptance. I had to hear about all the different dramas, fights, bullying and so on that had occurred while I was away. Jane had many home life dramas and she was in a social group at school but it didn't sound harmonious. I was pleased to have missed all the drama and I was entering back into school like a new kid. I would just naturally slot into Jane's clique.

CHAPTER 4

High School and First Love

I was pretty confused by teen drama and the social awkwardness I kind of felt not really attached to everyone's drama or the issues they had with each other. I had a fresh start and missed a good chunk of the social and acceptance battles that teens usually find themselves in for those first couple of high school years. I found I made friends easily and I was happy to talk to most. I even had a fairly good work ethic, always trying my best and respecting my teachers. I think I must have felt like I needed to be nice to everyone to be accepted and being just with my family for the last 14 months had taught me morals, patience and understanding. Finally, I had others besides my family to talk to.

When we had got back, I was supposed to have gone off to the local Catholic high school, but lucky for me, we were very broke and Mum was pregnant with my brother Jimmy. So, I had to go back to the Bronx school. I was happy because my friends went there. It didn't have a good reputation but I didn't care at the time. High school went fairly well. I met lifelong friends, had great teachers, experienced great teen life. My enemies were the naughty, mean kids. Some just didn't like people who worked hard or tried to do well. Some were probably seen as the popular girls, the ones who did drugs, had sex and roamed around the streets. There was also a bit of a low culture of girls getting pregnant to the local Aboriginal boys. It was seen to be cool or something and they would get benefits from the government for life. Anyway, it was people like this that were the ones I tried to stay clear of. There was a lot of violence on the streets of Lismore back then and it was not something most wanted to get involved in.

Just going to pause here in the past for a bit and pick it up again from here after I come back to present time.

So, since I started writing this ... I think I mentioned briefly my decision to abort my baby (fifth child). Well, that has happened and gone now. It's been about two months since I had a medical termination, meaning I took medication to stop and abort the pregnancy. I chose this option as I thought it would be less invasive and seemed like I could do it at home and not have to worry about my kids.

I had to have blood tests, an ultrasound and a clinic consult. Having the ultrasound and trying not to look at the screen, telling the lady I didn't want to know anything was awful. She however did want me to know I was having twins. OMG, so shit, not just one baby but two ... my heart broke. I couldn't stop crying. I left that appointment shocked but still knowing I couldn't do another baby, let alone two. I had intensely spoken to Mum about what was going on, what was I going to do? Both Mum and Dad agreed I could not do any more kids. My life was so chaotic with four already. I have pretty much done all the parenting by myself. My husband Antonio has not been around much, always off doing some sort of business venture, working six days a week, 14 hours a day, pretty much since our first son in 2009. My second son, Tristan, is autistic and he is intense. My third son, Leo, is also full-on with some sort of hyper disorder, yet to be diagnosed. Antonio was so shocked about this pregnancy and was straight away, "No, no, no, no, we can't do another." He has a hard time with the kids already and has had a bad 18 months of depression, bipolar and some personality disorder. He lost his business and basically hated life, including me, kids and people in general. Life with him at that point had not been easy and a lot of resentment had formed in our relationship.

Anyway, I knew I couldn't rely on him to suddenly step up and help out with new additions to the family. Mum and Dad made me realise that it wouldn't be fair on the other kids and I would not mentally come out of this well. So, my mind was made up. Mum came down to help me. She came to my consult and was with me the terrible night I took the last little pill to kill my babies. She cleaned my lounge when I bled through and made sure I was warm and my wine was topped up. We watched Jason Mamoa and sat up until 2am, and when the worst of it was over, I went to bed and cried a lot. Antonio didn't even come home that night and it broke my heart.

The next day the kids went off to school and day-care. Mum and I went and had coffee with my friends and took it easy for the day. I then had to organise Tristan's party; he was having about 40 people at Inflatable World. I was still bleeding heavily and was really sad. Antonio was mad, mean and abused me (verbally, emotionally) in front of my Mum. It was the saddest, loneliest week of my life. I couldn't believe I had married such a mean, selfish man. I felt in that moment we were done. I had been on anti-depressants for a couple of years, low dose to help me cope with my everyday stresses. My dose was not working anymore so I went back to the doctor to increase my meds. I didn't want to wish not to wake up in the morning anymore. I started my increased dose and I started not to be so sad. It took a big breakdown though, for me to go and get my dose increased, I felt ashamed I wasn't coping and that I needed more drugs to make me stronger.

I had a massive breakdown three weeks after my termination. I couldn't get up off the floor. I was so tired and emotionally I was exhausted. With me lying on the floor not being able to get up, not being able to keep it together anymore, Antonio was forced to snap out of his selfishness, and for a glimpse I saw the Ant I once knew, the man who gave a fuck about me. He had to take the reins for a bit, so I could lose it. After a few weeks it all settled down emotionally and we even organised our Easter long weekend away, kids too.

Anyway, back to the mid-1990s. I worked hard at school and I worked hard at my dancing. I had enrolled in a new dance school that opened in Lismore. All I had ever wanted to do was be a dancer, but I had just not had the opportunity to learn properly because no teachers were around at the time. A lady named Suzanna moved back to the Lismore area and she had been teaching and performing all over the world. Looking back, I can't say she was fantastic, but she enabled me to be creative, learn teaching techniques, as well as dance technique, took me to competitions, and nurtured my passion for dance. I soon started teaching for her on Saturday mornings and choreographing dances for concerts. I had a few part-time jobs as soon as I could get them, and dance teaching was one of them. I did my ballet exams and kept my eye on my goal of dance. I wanted to go to university for dance and was working towards that from Year 10. I did community projects, dance-related anything to give me experience. Drama was another subject I had interest in and I did school plays and did well in my drama for the HSC year.

I crushed on a few boys at school, although actually not my school. I had a boyfriend in Year 10 for about three months. He was really cute but a terrible kisser and a bit boring. I had fallen in love with a boy two years older than me. He had gone on my bus and he was quiet, bit shy but I thought he was gorgeous with blond hair that hung over his face and blue eyes. He had an old black Holden EH and he asked me out on a date. He only asked me out on a date after my little brother Dylan had told him I liked him on the bus, like told him every time he went on the bus. So maybe he felt he had to, to stop the little kid annoying him. It was so nerve-wracking and exciting. It was a daytime date. We went to the beach and for pizza in his car. He drove me to school a few times. Then he dumped me, and I was heartbroken. He was in Year 12 and had grand plans of a life in the big smoke of Sydney. He wanted to be an engineer and was planning on going to university, moving in with his brother who was already in Sydney living in Bondi. I was younger and not part of his plans, so we parted ways.

I went on a couple of dates with other boys but I never found a strong connection with them. I constantly thought of Daniel and I was probably a little stalkerish. I knew what he was up to most of the time. I had a friend through my job at the local club who was in his year at school and she and I had become very close. She knew of my Daniel obsession and kept me informed on his happenings.

It was around this time Years 10-11 that I had the best years of my life. I had a large circle of friends and ones that were different to each other and all moved in their own circles. I hung out with older kids and most were from the same school as Daniel. I went to great outings and had great times with friends around our area. Great parties and skinny dipping in the Whian Whian waterfalls after work on a Saturday night. My friend from work, Trish, was a really nice down-to-earth girl, and also a bit of a nerd and very trusted by my parents, and so as long as I was with Trish, Mum and Dad didn't seem to mind. I always called my parents and told them all my happenings. To the point where Dad told me to stop calling and yes, he would leave the key out for me.

I wasn't having sex. Yes, a little bit of drinking and doing silly things like driving a car without a licence, and I think I hitch-hiked once too, but I was pretty tame really, often the mother hen putting my drunk friends to bed. I had the whole time still been in love with Daniel. My friends got into pot smoking, but I never really liked it so I was often the straight one in the group.

I think it was around July in 1995, halfway through Year 10 that Daniel had been riding his motorbike to school. He always passed the back of my school on his way to his school. Right at the back of my school, he had a bad accident and ran into a turning trailer. I had been walking to our seat when I saw him trying to get up off the ground, swearing, collapsing. I tried to get to him and was rather distressed over the scene. The ambulance turned up and he was rushed off to hospital.

With the lack of mobile phones back then, it was hard to find out what or how he was doing. I had never met his parents but I had his home number, because of the good old White Pages phone book. The day after his accident, I rang his home number and spoke to his mum. I was so concerned that I didn't feel nervous or care what I might have been saying. I just introduced myself as a friend of Daniel and was very concerned for him wanting to know how he was doing. She told me of his broken bits and that he was in hospital for a few days yet. She thanked me for calling and I sent him my love.

When Daniel got out of hospital, he called me and we started talking again and he soon started turning up at work and waiting for me to finish so we could hang out. We started dating again and we were pretty happy. I let him do his HSC thing and tried not to be too needy at that time. He did really well in his HSC and got into his Aeronautical Engineering degree at a university in Sydney. We had a last date the day before he left to go to Sydney and I told him I loved him. He didn't reply... he got on his motorbike and I said I would write asap and he rode off. We were going to do the long-distance thing.

I went inside to cry my eyes out... already missing him.

It was pretty much three days later he called me from Sydney, telling me about his room and his enrolment day at university. It was then a week after that the first letter arrived. Long detailed letters, letters he usually wrote over a couple of days in lectures or on the bus. I longed for those letters and I got one or two a week from him along with two phone calls a week. It wasn't too long between visits either. He came home as often as he could and it was about six months into his Sydney life that he decided to defer for a year. He came home, showed up at my house and told me the news he was going to be around for about six months, work for his dad and hang out. Daniel's dad had a large macadamia plantation, and they lived only about five kilometres from me. Daniel was quietly spoken and never raised his voice. He had some weird friends but looking back now, I think they were probably a little a bit eccentric, nerdy and smoked too much pot. Daniel's parents were from Poland – very religious, at an older age bracket for parents and probably culturally a little different from me. Daniel was the youngest and I think his older sister babied him and his older brother was threatened by him being the younger, cuter one. Well, that's the feeling I got from them. His sister was always looking out for him and buying him things and then his brother would be arguing with him over little things or putting him down. Daniel was not a very affectionate person and held his emotions very close to him. He could not express himself properly and was uncomfortable with public affection. This would prove to be a constant issue in our relationship.

I like to think it was all me. I think he missed me and that was why he was coming home to stay a while. At this stage, I was halfway through Year 11 and we had a great, exciting relationship. I lost my virginity to him the night of his 19th birthday and I was 17. It was awkward. He had no idea (he was also a virgin) and I hadn't even seen a penis before. It was strange and not comfortable and I was confused for a bit. Daniel was from a strong Catholic background and he had a hard time with guilt about it. Anyway, we kept at it when we could and, eventually, we got better at it and we were comfortable with each other.

When the new year rolled around, he went back to Sydney and went back to Uni. I did my first visit to Sydney a few months into Year 12 and we did the long-distance thing. Daniel lived in an old terrace in Bondi Junction. His older brother lived upstairs. He worked in a bank and he always had this 'I think I'm too cool' attitude. He wasn't very nice to Daniel and the arguing continued. That first visit to Sydney, I remember his brother and Daniel picking me up from Central Station and taking me on a tour of the eastern suburbs. I couldn't go to pubs and clubs because I wasn't 18 yet so I spent the few days at his house and going to different food places trying food I hadn't eaten before. The old terrace house was old and I was a little shocked by the bachelor-ness of the house. It never seemed clean and everything was falling apart. It was years later that Daniel's brother had a party, a beach party and they filled the house with truckloads of sand. The floors were covered and the boys didn't care about how it was going to be cleaned, only that the scene was set for the beach party. It was a great party. The sand never really was properly removed though, it just added to the grit of the old house.

All my friends were having great times with their boyfriends or lack of and I started to get tired of the long-distance thing. A guy from school in a lot of my classes was writing me poetry, calling me, visiting and just being there. I used all my will power not to cheat on Daniel, and I never did. I broke Jed's heart and he wrote it to me in poetry. I was confused and probably led him on... wanting to be with him but not being able to, going to his house all the time, studying, singing with him. He was a fantastic guitarist and he helped me with my audition piece for Uni. Mum even cried once when we were rehearsing because she thought we should be together and the song had been so sad.

My friends were all starting to turn 18 and going out. I was going to a lot of parties and my older friends worked at changing my ID so I could go with them to the pubs. My family went on long holidays back up north and I was able to stay behind. Jane would move in with me at that stage and we would have people over. Jane's older brother spent a fair bit of time partying with us and his friends. He also helped us survive too, cutting firewood for us in the middle of winter and driving my cat to the vet when she had been bitten by a snake. Jane and I learned to drive at these times, bashing around the paddock in the paddock-basher cars. Until we were going a little fast one afternoon and the little four-wheel-drive went up on two wheels around a corner. We freaked out as it landed back on its four wheels. We turned the car off and walked away. When I got my L's and I had got a car, Jane and I would drive around the community, practising. We broke down one day, actually we ran out of petrol. We had to walk to a phone box really far away and call Jane's brother to come and get us. It was Daniel that taught me to drive properly when the time came. Dad tried, but I got too cranky with Dad when he tried to tell me how to do it.

I still went to school, work, dancing, and was still in a relationship with Daniel. I struggled a couple of times thinking I was letting a good thing go with Jed. I would break up with Daniel so I could try it out with Jed... but I could never stay broken up. Daniel came home a lot and at the end of the year, he was there for the three months of Uni break. He surprised me for my 18th birthday and showed up at my party. I had a great party on the farm. A paddock full of tents, hire toilets, dance floor, bonfire and all my childhood/teen friends were there. It was great, even though I did pass out by 10pm, woke up in a tent with no clothes on and no Daniel. People were asleep around the fire and sleeping on the dance floor... it looked like everyone had a great time. I cried because I had missed my 18th. Daniel had put me into the tent and gone home.

At the end of Year 12, my friends and I headed back to our favourite beachside town, Evans Head. We would go camping and stay for about two weeks. We had done this every year since Year 10 and had the best time hanging at the beach, running around with the locals, having beach parties every night. We would go back and forth to home for work. So many stories of those times and many adventures. We lived on noodles, hot chips, honey sandwiches and cheap sparkling wine. The end of Year 12 was our final year of doing this camp. It was a little different, as most had boyfriends. Most of the girl group had steady boyfriends and were settling into the next phase of our lives, waiting on Uni acceptances and HSC results. So, for this camp, we were probably maturing in our thoughts and it wasn't as much fun as we anticipated. What was to become of us now school was done?

While all my friends had gone off to Schoolies Week at the Gold Coast, I had done the audition process at a university in Brisbane for theatre and had stayed in Sydney and done my audition for university for dance. It was some time towards the end of our camping week that results and Uni offers came out. Daniel had gone home at this stage and I remember all us girls sitting outside our tent in the very early morning, 2am or something, waiting for the newspaper to be delivered to the local newsagency, where we would see our fate in print. Yep, that's how results were issued in those days.

The week before I had come away, I had already been offered a place in the Theatre course in Brisbane. It was only audition based, and I had made the cut out of 400 auditions where they only took a class of 25. It was very exciting. Jed was going to Brisbane and he had an early offer for Marine Biology. So, on this early morning at our tent, we sat around the newspaper while Sam (friend) went around the circle and read out everyone's offers. My heart was in two places. This was a major fork in my life's road. In Sydney, Daniel was there and dance was there. Brisbane had Jed and Theatre. I was really wanting a Sydney offer. Sam read out my offer for 1998 UWS BA in DANCE. I was so excited, scared and a little sad. I was moving to Sydney by myself in the big city… eek. The girls got their offers, and all were pretty much local so they would be going to Uni in Lismore or close. Jane was really upset as she had wanted an away offer but had been offered Tourism in Lismore. She hugged me and cried and then got angry I was going away. Her boyfriend was sitting with us the entire time and was clinging to her badly. He had been hoping for this result. He had an apprenticeship and wasn't going anywhere soon. He was banking on Jane being there with him. Jane flipped out on him then as she had enough of his clinginess and his plans for them to be stuck in Lismore forever. It was in that moment that she decided she was deferring and moving to Sydney with me. I hadn't asked her, but I was happy to have her with me for the next bit of our lives.

We had a great last summer in our home town, planning our future in Sydney. At the end of January 1998, Mum and Dad packed us up and we drove down to Sydney. I drove my car, and Mum and Dad drove the bus. We searched for a rental property for us when we got to Sydney, while I was at Uni orientation. That's when a rental unit was settled on and some op shop furniture was bought. Mum and Dad moved us into a two-bedroom ground floor unit in Kingswood (near Penrith). Rent was cheap and it was close to the new dance building I was going to be in for my second year.

Mum and Dad left after a few days and we began our new life...

CHAPTER 5

The Move to the Big Smoke: Sydney

I spent my five days a week going back and forth to Westmead on the train to UWS Westmead campus, where the dance course was. I was thrown into the course and it felt like a whole new way I had to learn to think. This was the beginning of my time as a dance artist. I embraced it whole heartedly, and worked hard to become a thinking dancer. The dance course back then was a full-time course and it really was a full-time thing. In that first year we had 35 in our class and we did not have time for a part-time job. Weekend rehearsals were also a thing. I loved studying dance and even though I was super poor, it didn't seem to bother me too much. Jane was in the same boat that first few months as she was on the dole. I remember eating a lot of rice meals and cereal with most of our money going to rent and utilities. My Nan gave me 100 dollars a month to help. This meant I was able to buy the occasional text book, ballet stockings or leotard. Sometimes, I admit, it went on a night out or a bottle of vodka for a Uni party.

I would often trek into the city after lectures on a Friday afternoon on the train. I would spend most of the weekend at Daniel's place in Bondi Junction. He had the front room in the old run-down terrace he shared with his brother and another roommate. Together, we were both pretty poor. He was in his second year of Uni doing Engineering and didn't have a part-time job. We often stayed home, watched movies, or went to the pub down the road for whatever specials they were running.

Daniel was difficult to get to come out west to my place. He was a bit of a snob like that and he started to get lazy in visiting me. We often fought about his lack of effort and money was also an issue, I guess. I started hanging out with my Uni friends a lot. Those girls were like family. We saw each other every day and had to spend many hours of classes and rehearsals together, so often we would just naturally have our down time together too. Sharing a passion for dance made us all close. Sometimes Daniel would meet me or tag along. My friends were probably a little full-on for him and we started to drift apart. In my second year of Uni I got a Sunday job at Wendy's, the ice-cream shop. The money really helped and I got to meet another great group of people.

A Uni friend, Kristy, was a major support for me through my early Uni days. We kind of stuck together. She was older and had grown up in the Western suburbs. She lived at home with her Mum and Dad. They were Spanish and I loved eating at her place and dancing at their family gatherings. We had a lot of fun together and her family sort of took care of me, fed me and gave me a bit of a family fix when I needed one. Kristy was a belly dancer and had lots of work around Sydney, I would often go with her to her gigs. She decided to teach me, so I could take her smaller jobs or when she had a double booking. It was pretty easy to learn and soon I was out dancing in restaurants earning good money. I was still with Daniel but I can't recall him being around much. Jane was still around too. She had a job at Wonderland, at a camera shop before that, had done part of a photography course, started an early education degree and had often been hanging with me in everything I was doing.

I had made some close friends at Uni and did a lot with them on weekends, sharing a passion for dance. I guess we as a year were always going to be close. Just realised I had already said that… anyway, it was in our third year of Uni that Jane and I wanted to move. We wanted a nicer street and a bit of a newer place. Our ground floor apartment in Kingswood was in a pretty bad area and we had junkies shooting up in our garage, had people peering in the windows and across from us was a very dirty and busy brothel. A friend from Uni was wanting to move out of her massive campus share house as she was having a hard time sleeping or getting to classes because the house was the party palace (it was an eight-bedroom European style mansion). Jane had made some friends at work and knew they were moving out of their three-bedroom townhouse which was about two kilometres away from our place in a much nicer location in Penrith.

It was the lead up to this move that my relationship with Daniel ended. I broke up with him over the phone. He wouldn't come to visit and we had a fight and I said, "Yeah, I'm done." It had been about three weeks earlier we had gone to visit his sister down in Jindabyne and had gone to a wedding of his friends. The weekend hadn't gone well. He had left me alone a lot at the wedding and his sister had been awkward, and he was unaffectionate and I felt he was being boring. So, with that still on my mind, I guess it was easy for me to break away. I still often think of Daniel, of course. He was my first love and thinking back, I was probably rather harsh on him. My personality was full-on and I liked a fast pace and fun. I was also a very affectionate person, which was uncomfortable for him. I'm friends with him on Facebook now and he got married a few years ago and just had his second child. I'm pretty sure he is happy.

My Nan, months before the Daniel breakup, had organised me a date. I don't like to call it a date, more like a meet and greet, with her friend's son who lived in Chatswood, who was an accountant. Nan knew my relationship with Daniel was fizzing out and she seemed to think Nigel the accountant would be a good match for me. I spoke a few times on the phone to Nigel before I organised a day visit out to his side of Sydney.

I met him at the train station and went to his apartment. We went for coffee, had lunch and he chatted most of the day... he loved his job and spoke about it a lot. I didn't feel a connection to him and was pretty keen to leave. I had a gig (belly dancing) that night so I used that as my excuse to escape. Nigel wanted to drive me to my gig. It was at a restaurant in Castle Hill, which was about halfway home. I told him after the gig I would have to train it home in the dark which I didn't want to do so I would rather go home, get my car and drive. I was also meeting friends at the Panthers Club for drinks after the gig. Nigel still insisted on driving me to the gig, then taking me to Panthers after that. He sat in the car while I did my 20-minute dance, showing no interest or perhaps a bit embarrassed to watch me, I think. He came across as fairly prudish.

After, we drove all the way out to Penrith to the Panthers Club. Nigel was a nice guy, I'm not saying he wasn't, but he wasn't really my type, I guess and we didn't have anything in common. He wasn't ugly, but he wasn't overly good looking either. Plain really, and a little overweight at the time. It came down to a lack of personality, and not the same interests at all. Anyway, we were signing in at the front desk at the club and it was super busy. A massive group of guys were signing in at the desk next to us. They were super loud, with a few ethnic looking guys in the group. I looked over at them and that's when I saw him...

It had been about four weeks earlier that I had attended a Uni party at 'the mansion'. A pimps and hoes dress up. Jane and I had gone together, and this other guy had been hanging around a bit – I can't remember his name. He had been trying really hard to impress me and had tried to kiss me a few times. Anyway, he wanted to come to this party too, so he did. Jane and I got drunk quickly and early on, and the guy clung to me badly, following me around and wouldn't leave me alone. I ran out into the backyard at some stage. I had taken off my stilettos when I was dancing... the house mates had turned the living room into a night club. I ran outside to get away from him and he was annoying me about something. Anyway, the backyard was full of bindies so I couldn't get far. I screamed then hit the ground on my bum. Yep, bindies then all in my arse. Some of my friends came out to pick them out of my butt, laughing hysterically with the guy trying to pick me up and me hitting him away in a drunken state, and my friends telling him to leave me alone.

I managed to get back inside, properly removed the bindies and the guy removed himself from the party. I poured another drink and went and stood in the long toilet line. The party toilet line was always a great place to chat and meet people. I started blabbing to a couple of girls and then to a guy that was also waiting in the line. He was really cute and spoke huskily to me about stuff (no idea what we were talking about). His name was Christian and his friend soon joined him in the line.

"Hey sexy red dress girl," (I was wearing a red dress) – that's how Christian's friend opened conversation with me.

I recognised the friend and had done a little stalking, as in pre-Facebook, pre-Insta stalking, like asking people about him. He was a Multimedia Design student, 21 years old, and his building was next to our new dance building. A couple of weeks earlier, his class had come into one of our dance classes to pick dancers for a photo shoot project they had to do. He did not pick me... he had picked a blonde second- year student. He had a bit of a reputation for being a bad boy and a slut. He had long dark hair, which he wore in a pony tail. He had dark eyes, wore really chunky shoes, lots of chunky silver jewellery and tight jeans. His name was Antonio and my friends had said he was not relationship material and only a fuck is what I would get from him.

So, on this mansion party night, he had noticed me. We started flirting and talking and I offered him a drink from my and Jane's vodka stash. The rest of the party was messy, and at some stage I passed out in the pass-out room (a room full of girls mainly, very drunk and not well, sleeping it off). I had a little spew, a sleep and woke trying to crawl out of the dim room over the bodies. I managed to get to the door and as I reached the doorway, a pair of shoes I recognised stood in my way... "Ant," I called as I hugged his feet.

He lifted me off the ground. "Wondered what happened to you," he said as he helped me down the stairs. We met Jane on the stairs.

"Where've you been?" she asked accusingly, death-glaring Antonio in the process. It was at that point Antonio put handcuffs on me and took off downstairs with me. Jane followed, trying to get me away from the man that had handcuffed himself to me. Jane in the end declared that we were going home and demanded the handcuffs be removed now. Antonio did release me, but not before propping me against the wall and getting my phone number. He then walked us out to my car and Jane drove us home, Antonio saying he would call me.

So back to the club front desk, me with Nigel signing in and Antonio with a large group of his friends at the desk next to us. I saw him but pretended not to and I could feel him staring at me and Nigel. My heart was pumping hardcore. I was angry at him, though. He hadn't called me so I assumed he wasn't interested. I walked off with Nigel to the sports bar, ordered a drink and sat at a table talking. Half an hour into our sitting, I got up to go to the bar and get another drink. When I returned there was Antonio sitting in my seat chatting to Nigel... eek WTF! When I sat down, Antonio turned his focus to me. He freaked out Nigel, I remember, and sometime soon after that Nigel said he had to go and he could drive me home now. Antonio told him not to worry and that he would get me home. Nigel wasn't comfortable with that. I walked Nigel to his car, explaining it was okay, my friends would be here soon and I knew Ant from Uni so he wasn't a stranger. I thanked him for the day and the lift to Penrith and said I would chat to him soon.

I then walked back into the Panthers Club and joined Ant and his friends. My friend Kristy turned up after her belly dancing gigs and joined in the all-night socialising. We stayed at Panthers until the morning. Kristy dropped me home in time for me to shower and get my uniform for Wendy's. I struggled all day at work but was on a massive high from last night's fun and seeing Ant. I was so tired and ready to sleep when I got home that afternoon. Ant called me at 5pm telling me he was coming to pick me up to go on a proper date. Dinner and a movie. Don't really remember the movie. We talked a lot and then went to the river to make out. I wouldn't sleep with him because I hadn't broken up with Daniel at this stage. It was pretty much that week that I did call it quits with Daniel.

Antonio came around a lot, bought me lots of things, took me to dinners and brought a heap of excitement and fun to my life. He was mysterious, a little possessive and protective and when we did have sex it was different, scary at first but exciting. He was generous in and out of the bedroom and he was completely different to anything I had ever known. I fell in love with him quickly, but did not tell him. It wasn't until the Christmas party at our unit a few weeks before we were to move, Ant had been in the picture for about two months and he told me he loved me first.

Kristy told me I was stupid to get involved with him. We were never the same again as friends after that. She became a bully towards me and created a lot of drama with nasty comments and leaving me out of social things. I stayed civil to her until the end of Uni. She had a way of manipulating people so I needed to stay on her good side and that's what I tried to do. I had witnessed her meanness a lot during our friendship but she had not been that way with me because I was a loyal friend to her. I was probably a bit of a Kristy servant, always doing things for her and with her. If she asked me to jump, I probably said, "Sure, how high?" I must have been scared of her, I think. A people pleaser, always trying to keep the peace and make others happy. Chasing that validation for existing, I definitely recognise that trait in me now and something I'm still working on today.

Antonio and his friends helped us move into our new townhouse and it was all like a new start. The final year of my dance course was approaching, I had a new man and I felt loved, wanted, desired, and that my life was about to get exciting. Ant was very creative and took a lot of photos of me. He painted and he played guitar. We went out a lot and he met my parents. I met his family. We went on a holiday to my home town and had a week at the Gold Coast in a swish hotel, something I had never experienced before. My parents were wary at first because he was so different to our usual kind of people and Mum and Dad were a little concerned that he was a bad boy. However, a year into our relationship, my family loved Ant. He had a way of engaging people and knowing how to be relatable. My siblings loved him and hung on every word he said.

He was always willing to help in any way he could. Ant threw me a 21st birthday at a local Masonic Centre. He paid for the whole thing and invited everyone we knew, and my family came down for it. My younger brothers and sister were the bar servers. They were all under age and ended up quite drunk by the end. My brother Dylan spewed everywhere. All my friends came and it was a great night.

We were dressed up in a Masquerade Ball theme. This was our final year of our dance degree and we were preparing to tour and going our separate ways soon. Some were going on to do education to be dance school teachers. I didn't want to do that. I wanted to be a dancer and choreographer.

I had started doing dance shows, in clubs, Madonna tributes, cabaret dancing, and anything else dance show-like. At the completion of the dance degree, I kept at the shows and picked up choreography work and dance studio teaching. At the start of my first year out, I sent a letter out to dance studios in Sydney offering myself for teaching work. That's how I started my regular dance teaching job at TANIA's STRICTLY DANCING (TSD). I started teaching for Tania about three days/afternoons a week and Saturday mornings. I stayed with Tania for 14 years. I was able to have other jobs and still dance in the afternoons. I started a retail job with Bloch dance shop in Liverpool, learnt how to fit pointe shoes and sell anything dance-related. I was able to work my way up through Bloch and in my second year I was Store Manager in the new Penrith store, all the time still doing my dance stuff on the side. I even managed to get a paid contemporary dance gig monthly at The Tap Gallery in Paddington.

My dancing hadn't gone completely to plan. I got ripped off a few times, not getting paid and shows being cancelled. I had auditioned for Moulin Rouge but that was a joke, really. I only stand at 5'5" maybe. The lady laughed at me, saying, "Oh, you're a cute little thing, when I need a show with short people, I will let you know." I convinced myself I wouldn't have been able to leave Ant anyway and carried on teaching and working.

I had become pretty obsessed with wanting to get married. I felt like I was living in limbo. Ant had been working but was still living at home. He had a few different jobs in his industry and also dabbled in his own businesses. We had been together three years, I think, by the time he decided he was going to buy a restaurant in Bondi. I was still living with Jane in the townhouse. Our other roommate had lasted a year with us then she had moved back home after Uni for a bit. Ant didn't like talking about getting married much. He had said yes, he wanted to, but not until he was secure financially, so all I could do was try to be patient. Ant's first Bondi restaurant was soon to open. It was on the main beach, a little contemporary Italian. It was a great restaurant and I loved going there most weekends, taking my friends and eating and drinking by the beach.

CHAPTER 6

The Visit!

I was getting pretty pissed with the no marriage thing. All my friends were getting married and with each wedding I went to, I got sadder and madder. That's why I decided to do something I had been longing to do. I decided to go travelling around Australia. I coaxed my brother Leon to come with me. He was into the outdoors. He was still living at home at that stage and was finishing up his plastering apprenticeship. I bought a little 4x4 Pajero IO and started collecting everything we would need. I kept working and saving for 12 months. I put in for four months leave with work and dancing. I travelled up to Lismore, had a couple of days collaborating with Mum and Dad about the journey and how to pack the car properly. Dad had a special roof rack made to attach to the car so we could take a little tinny (boat) with us.

My brother Leon was/is a really quiet guy. He had been hurt a lot in life, didn't trust many people and didn't have a great relationship with our step mum. Mum had been rather strict with my brothers and sister most of the time and the fallout from that had been an emotional wall and resentment. Leon had also never asked about or spoke about our real Mum. He reckons he wasn't interested and just didn't care. So, it was our journey that set the way for me to bring back my brother, make him feel better, try and explain things to him, have some conversations about feelings and our real mum too.

It had been a few years before this trip, actually just after my 21st birthday. Our real mother, Diana, had contacted Dad and wanted to have a visit with us all at her place in Tweed Heads. She would randomly write letters to Dad over the years. The letters wouldn't make much sense, often talking about aliens and Dad painting a yellow submarine. In this letter it had been about the same stuff but also about how she wanted to see us. I had been reluctant but thought that as so many years had passed, perhaps it would be better. My sister had always wanted to see her and felt she had all her life been missing a proper mother-daughter relationship. Leon was not interested and Tom had no clue about much at all as he was only a newborn when it all went to shit.

We went to visit Diana. I travelled up to Lismore to meet the family and all my siblings were there Leon, Summa, Tom. We went to her house which was a group house for people with mental disabilities. Dad and Mum took us and we stopped out the front. Dad was worried. He was not liking this at all. He wanted to come with us, and I so wanted him to, but this was not his battle anymore. He had been through enough with Diana over the years and I didn't want him to have to go through this.

"No, Dad, we need to do this ourselves. Just don't leave us here too long and keep your phone on in case."

Diana walked out... and down the driveway to meet us as we got out of the car. She was unrecognisable. She looked old, overweight and had a lesbian-looking haircut. Gone was her beauty but her vacant stare was still there, still cold dark eyes.

Her eyes looked us up and down and then went to Dad. "Wow, good to see you, you haven't changed."

"Hi Di... Okay, I will be back in about two hours, two-and-a-half hours, yeah?" Dad said, looking at me. I nodded.

"Come in, my darlings, can't believe youse are here," she said, starting to walk up the driveway into the house.

I started to follow and my siblings kind of stood there not moving, with an almost shocked, shy, dumb look on their face. I gave them the big sister bossy eyes and they started to move. Tom was the only excited and smiling one out of us... he almost skipped into the house. Leon shrunk into the background and Summa was hopeful. I turned back to watch Dad, Mum, Jimmy and Dylan drive away. I felt sick.

We entered the house and the screen door closed behind us. Diana had been chatting the entire time… I started to tune back in and she was telling Summa a story about how the aliens had stolen her spine when she was a baby. Shit. Summa was freaking out, looking to me for an explanation. I gave her the crazy around the ears hand signal with the crazy eyes, and think she understood what I was getting at. Tears sprung to her eyes. Diana soon moved on to Leon, talking about how he had been the most perfect baby, that he was her beautiful baby boy, blah blah. Leon was dying, he couldn't stand it and she kept asking him to hug her and kept touching his face. Leon even kept pushing her hands away. He moved to me and stood next to me like I could protect him or something. We walked to the back of the house into a really large kitchen area. That's when we saw the gathering of people in the kitchen, some looking vaguely familiar, but still strangers. The strangers stepped towards us; I think there were about five of them. A tall, blonde skinny lady I recognised as Aunty … She gushed and carried on about how good it was to see us etc.

I'm a bit vague myself on the others that were there that day. I know our grandmother was not, as she had passed away about ten years earlier from breast cancer. I know our grandfather wasn't there either because he had been banned from the family. The family, I think, had given up on him after Grandma J had died. He had been an abusive alcoholic and there had not been a day that had gone by in their marriage that Grandma J had not been bashed around by him. She had lost her life to cancer but she had not had a great life anyway and her suffering stopped when she died. Grandma J, I do remember, was a really kind bubbly human and I felt nothing but love for her. I was always excited to see her. She sang songs and played with me a lot as a little one. She was picked on by Diana and she was generally not treated well by any of her family. I know she also was a heavy drinker and started drinking a lot more as her years progressed and I would guess it was to numb her life and get her through the days.

He (Grandpa C) was never charged for domestic abuse and never dobbed in for the sexual abuse to his daughters either. I only have a vague memory of him. He was an overweight, sweaty man, missing teeth and with an overly creepy presence to him. So, I think I could say I was happy he was not among the people that were there that day. He died many years later alone and in a nursing home. Diana went on and on about crazy stuff, ramblings of memories she had of us and memories of things that had not happened but seemed real to her mind. Her attention came to me at times in the conversation and I was met with her cold eyes and a hatred in her voice. She didn't have a funny memory of me. She didn't have one nice, loving thing to say about me. I felt like I was back to being a five-year-old and emotionally abused again. I could feel myself shutting down. We had been there for half an hour maybe when I tried to call Dad to come back and get us. Dad's phone was out of range or no service… I tried five times and it went straight to message bank.

Diana and the strangers had now pulled out a heap of crap food, lollies, cake and soft drink. We were there for lunch, and this was going to be it. Tom was over-excited, stuffing his face with cake and hugging Diana like he knew who she was. I stuck close to Leon and Summa and tried to help them answer questions or explain her actions to them. We were stuck there. I kept trying to call Dad but he had no service. I left a message and then another. After close to three hours, Dad knocked at the door and we all rushed to the door to meet him. Leon opened the door and started to walk to the car, without Dad. Dad apologised. He was so sorry he had no reception then when he did check his messages he came straight away, but they were over the other side of Gold Coast by then.

Diana walked to the front door gushing and blahing on with crazy shit. I said goodbye with a tight smile, trying to hold back tears. Summa gave her a brief hug and Diana chased after Leon calling him beautiful boy. Leon stopped at the car, waved to her and jumped in the car, closing the door before she reached him. Tom hugged her longingly, called her mummy and then also walked to car. We were safe in the car and tried to not look at each other. Dad did the small talk thing with Diana and also said goodbye, got in the car and we drove off. No one spoke for about five minutes until we were around the corner and away. I started to cry and sob badly. Mum asked what happened... I couldn't get it out and could not explain it. Leon piped up. "That lady crazy." Dad pulled the car over near the river and we all got out and talked about the experience. We also agreed that day that we would not be seeing Diana again.

I haven't seen her since that day and she kind of dropped off the radar for five years or so. She wrote another crazy letter to Dad at some stage that made no sense. She did say she had remarried and lived in a caravan park somewhere in Queensland. She had both her breasts removed and was recovering from breast cancer. It wasn't too long ago in real time, as in now, that we discovered we had a heap of half-brothers and sisters.

One of the half-brothers made contact with my brother, Jimmy, recognising the last name on Facebook, asking if he had a mother named Diana. Jimmy passed him onto me knowing what he was looking for. We learnt from this brother that Diana had gone on to have at least five other children after us. All of them had been taken from her and she had even tried to kill one of her babies in the bath. The brother that contacted us was the youngest of them. He had just turned 18 and he wanted to know more about his real mum. He had been adopted out to the same family that three of the others had also. Each of the kids had different fathers and knew not much about Diana, except that she was mentally not well. He told us that he was the baby that Diana had tried to drown in the bath. He says he knew this because he had been given a letter that was given to his adopted parents on his adoption and she was apologising for trying to kill him.

Anyway, we went and met up with him Brisbane in 2017. The other siblings (his full and my half) were meant to come too but at the last minute they did a no-show. Leon, Summa and I had travelled all the way to Brisbane to meet them but only he showed. We still have contact with them all via social media but that's about it.

CHAPTER 7

Hit the Road Again

So, it wasn't long after the meeting Diana again experience that Leon and I set out on our great Australian adventure. We headed north that first day in April (can't remember the date, possibly 2003). We had our first night on the road at Gympie, Queensland. We stayed at a rest stop by the road, free camping. Leon set up my tent for me and he used his swag on the ground. I cooked dinner on my camp stove, we had a couple of beers, and it was that first night I made Leon talk about stuff and open up a bit. We listened to Cold Chisel a lot on that trip. There were long drives, long silences but we were comfortable with each other and generally happy to be travelling and seeing Australia. Leon was itching to be a little dangerous and take a few more risks than me. He was younger, single and the car wasn't his... I was a bit of a worrier and I think it probably started to annoy him.

We went up to Weipa. Nan and Pop were up there for their three months of the year that they always did every year. The road was 600 kilometres of corrugations and washed-out dirt road. Leaving from Cairns, it took us two and a half days to get there. The boat rack had rattled loose and we had to tie the boat with rope from under the chassis up to the roof. We spent the last day of the Weipa trip holding the boat on with our hands... it was a long, hard, stressful drive.

We got to Weipa and set up camp next to Nan and Pop's van. It was great fishing in Weipa at the time and we had a great week with Nan and Pop, fishing, prawning, crabbing. Pop and Leon were similar in what they liked to do in the outdoors and they were men of few words. I enjoyed Nan's company and Leon and Pop enjoyed theirs. We left Weipa with a heavy heart. We were meant to go on north to Cape York but we weren't able to get the boat properly secured to the roof, so we had to head back to Cairns. We did the trip slowly and when we hit the sealed road on the other end, we were happy we had made it.

On the way up to Cairns, we hadn't stopped at our beloved Wonga Beach (north of Port Douglas). The weather had been way too wet so we had just kept on to Weipa. So, we now headed to Wonga. We were excited. Leon was super excited about his happy place... it is also our Dad's happy place. We would go to Wonga almost every year, fishing, diving, cray fishing. We would stay in the caravan park there which was a tiny little paradise under the coconut trees on the beach. The boat was on the beach. We could walk down the beach into the tinny and out to the reef, diving every day.

So, this is where Leon and I set up camp for the week. We had the little tinny on the beach just like we would have if Dad was there. We went out diving, went up the Daintree, put in crab pots and would go prawning on the beach at night. Every night, the people of the caravan park (oldies) would meet at the Manager's van and happy hour would go for hours. Leon and I would go every day at 5pm, sometimes we'd take some seafood that we had caught to share around with the oldies. It was great times. Leon and I were the youngest there and we loved hearing the stories and dirty jokes from the Wonga oldies. Wonga Beach is a stretch of coconut-lined beach that lies between Mossman (north of Port Douglas) and the mouth of the Daintree River. Just off the beach is reef that is full of painted crayfish. A short boat ride north takes you to the mouth of the Daintree and east will take you to Snapper Island. Snapper Island's beach doesn't really have sand. The beach is made of smoothed down coral and it's a great place to dive out there too. Although today you would probably need to try and dodge the crocodiles.

From Wonga, when our week was up, we packed up sadly and started our trip to Karumba, across the tip to the gulf. It was a long, hot drive with not much to see and when we got to Karumba, we were disappointed. It was really hot and like a ghost town, a sandy ghost town. We had wanted to fish the gulf, but it was really rough and we weren't going to put the tiny tinny in. We fished off the rocks and caught nothing. We stayed I think two nights, then decided to move on, nothing much for us to do. From Karumba, we moved on to Mount Isa, again a long drive. When we got to Mount Isa, we set up camp in a caravan park on the outside of town. We set up our camp, planning to stay just the night. Next to us were two backpacker boys. I was cooking our dinner and Leon was sitting having a beer. I started some small talk with our new neighbours. They were eating green apples for dinner as they were so poor and couldn't afford a meal. I invited them to eat with us… can't remember what we were having, but they were happy. They moved their chairs over to our camp and we talked, laughed and shared a couple of beers until rather late. Lenny and Jonno were their names. They were from London and had been in Australia for nine months. They were traveling to Perth in a beat-up old Ford.

The next morning, we had breakfast together and started chatting about our plans while we packed up. They were heading the same way as us and we decided we would travel together until WA. It was exciting to have some travel companions and now in numbers, I was more confident to do more bush camping. We stopped, got some supplies and started out of Mount Isa into the unknown, heading to the NT border. That first day we drove about seven hours with them following us. We stopped at roadhouses for fuel and then beer at the last one. After a couple more hours of driving, Leon turned off the road to follow a desert track… the boys followed and we found a dried-up creek bed protected from the wind. We set up camp, collected wood and started to settle in. It was just before dark when Lenny decided they didn't have enough beer and would need to go get more from back at the roadhouse two hours away. Leon and Lenny took my car and left... Jonno and I stayed, got the fire started and then about an hour after the boys had left it got dark. It got very dark. We sat around the fire and as it kept getting blacker and blacker, we moved closer to the fire and I held tight to our only light. Jonno and I talked a lot. I learnt a lot about him and I thought he was gay. Apparently, he was not... anyway, we were a little scared, I think. The darkness, the nothingness of where we were was eerie.

Sometime after 8pm, we saw the car lights coming through the scrub... they were back. Leon was driving and came screaming through. Lenny jumped out of the passenger side holding half a carton of beer. Cans fell out onto the dirt... driving back on the long trip had seen them drink half the carton. We then felt comfortable and we all started drinking and talking around the fire. I remember that night, the stars were amazing. We were the only people out there for hundreds of kilometres.

I won't go into the whole trip as it would take too long and probably be a bit too boring. I had kept my rented townhouse back in Penrith while I was away. My sister and cousin moved in with Jane to help pay rent and live the Sydney life for a while. Antonio paid my bills while I was gone – phone, car and emergency money if I needed. Leon and I had a few fights when we were travelling with the backpacker boys. He wanted to be reckless and didn't care that my car was going to die if we went certain places. They wanted to be adventurists or something and put us at risk to get a thrill. I wouldn't because I wanted to make the trip in one piece and be able to get home. It was becoming a bit of a boys' club at times. I remember on our way to Alice Springs, the boys were happy free camping every night. We had done four nights just pulling off the highway following a track into the desert, setting up camp, collecting firewood etc.

In the nights it would get freezing in the desert and we looked pretty homeless in our many layers, sleeping in hiking boots. I longed for a warm shower by night four, and said to the boys that tomorrow night I needed a shower and to do washing, so we have to stay in a caravan park. The boys went on stupid calling me a princess and that I was being boring, and who cares what you look like or smell like. They upset me that night and I went off a little, and they told me to calm down. I gave them the "I'm a woman" spiel and I have needs, those needs of the hygiene kind. Lenny looked at me like, "WTF are you talking about."

I explained, "Well, if I go one more night without a shower or a toilet, my womanly issues will be attracting the dingoes from the stench and we will all be mauled to death."

"What womanly issues, huh?" Lenny questioned. Then it obviously dawned on him judging by a look of shock on his face. "Sorry, sorry, yeah for sure, showers tomorrow."

I got my caravan park the next two nights and all was okay.

We broke down in Kakadu when we went down a four-wheel-drive only track. The boys didn't have a four-wheel-drive, but they insisted. It was getting dark and we had wanted to get to the falls where the campground was also. The track was bad but we had made it 10 kilometres and only had 5 kilometres to go when we got to a river crossing. It looked deep and kind of boggy. Leon got out and walked it, fell into some holes and was trying to walk better paths we could take. We could hear a car coming from the other side. Leon got out of the way... it was a yellow Jeep. The Jeep got a run up (they had obviously been through before) and floored it through the river... but on the way up on our side, they hit a sand mound and got stuck. They tried to get the car to move but the wheels were spinning. The people got out of the car to check the damage and work it out. Leon and the boys tried to push, but it was stuck. I offered my car and snatch strap to snatch them out. Leon attached the two cars to the snatch strap, gave some slack and floored the little IO. The Jeep moved a little... he did it again and with a crash and a bang, the Jeep popped out. The crash and bang was our boat flying off the top of the car, ripping the roof racks fully off my car.

The Jeep people were so grateful. They were doctors on holidays and they needed to get back to their accommodation. My snatch strap was now stuck to their car and it wouldn't come off. It was right on dark now and we were stuck... we could not drive my car. The doctors took my address so they could send my snatch strap back to me. Before they left us by the track in the middle of Kakadu, they wanted to know if we wanted the ranger to come get us... did we need rescuing? We decided no, we would try and put the rack back on, camp here the night and leave in the morning. We set up camp in the bush only about 10 metres back from the track. Leon and Lenny worked on the racks and got the boat reattached, sort of. The flies were super bad and then the mozzies extra bad as it got darker. That night sleeping in my tent, I was pretty scared. Before bed, we had sat around our light and the sounds of the dingoes were loud. When we shined a torch out into the dark, we were surrounded by eyes. The backpacker boys didn't know much about dingoes and somehow Leon had convinced Lenny to sleep in his swag, and Leon was going in the tent.

That night we were woken by Lenny going crazy. "Aaagghh, fuck off, fuck off!" He was tipping a bucket of water over himself. A dingo had been sniffing his head and then all over him, he freaked out and screamed to scare it off. I don't know why the water over his head, though. We were super happy to leave there in the morning.

We had many adventures with our backpacker friends. Their car broke down a lot, ran out of oil a lot. We made our way through the Northern Territory, and met lots of other travellers. We swam with fresh water crocodiles, went to hot springs, climbed Ayres Rock (Uluru), climbed Kings Canyon (Leon did it in thongs, another thing we had a fight about. It was not safe to climb cliffs in thongs, was my argument). We travelled over to WA to Kununurra with the boys. Leon had run out of money so I was now paying for everything and had worked out I had enough money to get us home, but quickly, so two weeks to get home, only stopping over nights.

So, after a few days in WA, Leon and I said goodbye to the boys after three months of travelling with them. It was sad to say goodbye. Leon and I started the journey home.

CHAPTER 8

Marriage or Bust

I arrived back to Sydney after almost five months away, feeling I had done what I had always wanted to do. I felt more grounded and like I had seen the world... even though it was only Australia. My sister and cousin moved on when I got back, and life resumed pretty quickly to pre-travels. I went back to work at Bloch and went back to Tania's Dancing. Within a few months of being back, I got offered a higher position at work and became Visual Merchandiser for Bloch, travelling to all the stores to sell merchandise.

Antonio's Bondi restaurant was going well and he was living in Bondi through the week with his business partner. He was sleeping on the floor in a studio apartment that was filthy. He would go home on Sundays, drop off washing and come see me and usually stay Monday nights with me. We were basically doing a long-distance relationship and were lucky to see each other once a week.

At some point Ant moved into his own disgusting Bondi studio apartment. An old 70's building. It was pretty grubby. I would sometimes drive all the way in after work and stay. I had got my dog, Penny, by now. She was a puppy and I had searched for her for a while. Ant bought her for me and I got a new car the same week, a bright blue Toyota Echo. Jane hated my dog... Penny was a bit of a naughty puppy and very noisy at night. I used to take Penny with me everywhere, she would come stay at Ant's, she taught herself to pee over the shower drain and pooed on the one-person balcony. She did, however, destroy the bed, carpets and anything she could when we were at work.

I had a few job changes around this time, working for different companies – Merchandising, Managing. At the beginning of 2004, March I think, Ant organised us a day out to the Hunter Valley. He organised a white stretch limo to take us on a wine tour for the day. I straight away thought he was going to propose. I had been sooking about it for a while and it had only been the Christmas past that Dad had words to him about hurrying up.

However, when the limo arrived and my excitement showed, he cut me down quickly. "Not what you think, it's our last day together for a while so wanted to make it a good one."

Ant was about to open his second restaurant, so days off were no more for a bit. I was pretty cut about that. We travelled the two hours up to the Hunter and spent the day wining the day away. Our last cellar door of the day was Audrey Wilkinson, a great winery, great views. We were both pretty drunk by then and decided we were going to run through the vines. Glass of wine in hand and my shoes in the other, we walked through the vines.

Ant was not really liking all the wine and was having a a whinge about it, then said to me, "Gee your wine is sparkly."

I didn't really listen... I had a swig of my wine.

"No, look at it!" he yelled.

I looked at my glass, a bit annoyed by his outburst. Then I saw the ring in the bottom of the glass, I had almost drunk it! A beautiful one-carat diamond solitaire.

He got down on his knee and asked me. "Nikki Stein, will you marry me?"

I cried and I put the ring on. "I gotta call Mum and Dad."

"But you didn't answer me. Is that a yes?" he asked.

I cried some more and said yes. It was very romantic, and thinking back to that moment brings tears to my eyes. The happiness and the hope of the future were so promising and exciting to wonder about. The Antonio of then was such a different person. Romantic, and so full of expectations and plans for life. For the year to come, we planned and worked for our wedding.

We searched for a house, we booked our wedding, we found an apartment in Waterloo in the city. It had a ground floor garden, perfect for Penny. We had an engagement party, actually, we had two – one in Sydney, one in Lismore. I sorted most of the wedding details and I even got re-baptised so we could do the Coptic Orthodox thing for the wedding.

The year went by in a blur, really, and two months before the wedding, we moved into our apartment. Then we did our hens' and bucks' weekends. A few days before our wedding, my family arrived. Mum and Dad stayed with us and on my side the rest of them (Aunties, Nan etc.) all stayed at a hotel in Paddington. We had hired a bus/coach to pick them up from there on the day of the wedding. The night before the wedding, Ant went to his parents and I went to The Log Cabin, a motel in Penrith. I went with Mum, Dad and my bridesmaids. We stayed in Penrith because my hairdresser was out there and the florist. We had a nice relaxing night leading up to the wedding day.

On May 8th 2005, Ant and I got married. We had a huge wedding of 230 guests — it was a wonderful party and my family still talk about it being the best wedding they had ever been to. We had it at Dockside Darling Harbour overlooking the harbour. We had great food, our friend's band playing along with a DJ and Arabic music too. It was great. Antonio and I were happy though, for it to be over. We wanted the honeymoon. We left the next day to the Hunter Valley for three days then back to Sydney to catch our flight to Tahiti, where we did an eight-night cruise around Tahiti. Life was so good, and we were very happy.

When we returned from our honeymoon, I went back to work at a Boutique at Bondi and Ant went to his new shop in Bondi Junction. However, his business partner had changed the locks and taken a heap of money. He had pushed Ant out within two weeks of him not being there. This dragged on for a while, and in the end, Ant walked away with nothing. Lost everything. He went and got a job as a coffee rep. We carried on our city life. I bused it to work most days and drove out to the Hills District to teach dance three days still. We were happy. Our first year of marriage came and went. We went on holidays, had friends over a lot and made new friends.

It was within that first year of married life that we met Glen and Sandy. They were a couple that lived in the same complex. I met Glen while I was walking Penny in the middle grounds of the complex. He also was walking a beagle, so we got chatting. He came to our place for drinks one afternoon and stayed for dinner. His partner, Sandy, was a General Manager of a high-end ladies clothing company, and she was overseas. It was a couple of months before I got to meet Sandy, but when I finally did, I knew she was a 'me' person. We had a connection straight away. Sandy did become my boss when I started to work for her as National Merchandising Manager. I flew everywhere around the place, and got to wear all the great clothes Sandy designed for free. I was still able to keep dancing too.

CHAPTER 9

Andrew and the Ones that Got Away!

Antonio and I, after our first-year anniversary, decided we were going to try and start a family. So, I came off the pill and started to try. Nothing happened and when it came around to our second anniversary and we were not pregnant, I went off to start the investigations of how come? I had some check-ups, checked my tubes, ovaries, blood tests, ultrasounds, etc. Nothing strange to report. Then Ant went to be checked out also, and nothing strange there either. After a few more months of no reasons, we signed up for IVF. We started to visit the IVF clinic in Maroubra and we entered the first phase of treatment. Back then, I remember the cost was high and I think we borrowed the money to do it. I had injections every day, which Ant gave me in the stomach. When it would get to around day ten, I would have to go to the clinic every morning to have ultrasounds to see if my eggs were ready to ovulate. When they were ready, we would then have to come back the next morning with Ant's swimmers in a cup, nice and warm, ready to be put into me.

We did this round twice and then I fell pregnant. The excitement of the phone call that I received from the clinic made me feel giddy. There was no better/happier feeling. At around the six-week point, we went to get a scan to check. There was a pregnancy. Our three-year anniversary came so we decided to go to Fiji. We were so happy and excited about expecting. I took it easy in Fiji, drank juice, didn't go horse riding, and just lazed around. We did five days in Fiji and then came home to our next appointment. Another ultrasound to check heartbeat. We went into the Randwick Hospital ultrasound clinic and we were excited to see the baby now.

The ultrasound guy went internally to get a proper look. "There's no heartbeat," he explained. "The pregnancy is not viable. I'm sorry."

It looked as though the foetus had died about a week earlier. I was going to miscarry. I cried so much... we sat in the clinic room for a long time. I didn't want to leave there because I wasn't sure how to go on from here. Our IVF doctor called us while we sat in the clinic, asking what I wanted to do. He offered me to have a DNC the next day if wanted it over now or I could wait to miscarry. I decided to get it done the next day.

I walked out of that appointment that day and I know looking back now, I was never the same again. It's a point I can pinpoint in my life that changed me. Life was never good anymore, it was hard to see the light, it was hard to feel joy. It would be many more tries and IVF courses before we fell pregnant again. We had moved out to Glenmore Park about a year later. We had sold our apartment and I had lost my job because the company was folding. Sandy and Glen were losing their jobs too. Ant and I kept going to the clinic in Maroubra. I fell pregnant almost exactly a year after my first loss. We had moved into a massive three-storey mansion. It hadn't been properly finished and Ant couldn't sell it. It was meant to be an investment property but we moved into it after we sold the apartment. I liked the idea of being back out in my old stomping ground. I got a job as a store manager at a high-end shoe and accessories store at Castle Hill. It was nice and close to dance too.

Anyway, during the next pregnancy I was so scared. I went for regular scans and everything was doing okay. Then at about nine weeks, I started to bleed. I made an appointment at the ultrasound place and he confirmed I was miscarrying again. He made my appointment right then and there for me to have a DNC. I can't remember if I went that afternoon or the next day. I do remember the shower after it, Ant helping me in at home. I couldn't stand up, I was inconsolable. Ant didn't know what to do or say anymore, it so consumed our lives. I had another miscarriage but I can't remember much of that one. I know we got to the three-year mark of trying, that our IVF doctor told us to have a break. He said there was no reason for it to not be working for us but we should have a break. We had reached the egg retrieval stage. They had planted three embryos in three different courses and none had survived. Our other five embryos hadn't survived the thawing process. So yes, it was time for a break.

We tried to go about normal life. I sought advice from herbalists and even visited a spiritual healer. I did feel better and hopeful after the healer. She pointed me in the direction of a man named Eli, an iridologist. Ant was concerned for me. He saw I wasn't the same person anymore. I cried all the time and was always negative. He dropped me at my psychology appointments and took me to the healer. His friend's mum had been to her and it had helped her a lot, so he was hopeful for me that the healer would help. We had been running late for the healer's appointment, stuck in traffic. It was a Tuesday night after work. Ant dropped me at the front and was driving around to get parking. I walked up the dark stairs to the consult room. It was above a restaurant in the main street of Leichardt. I pushed through the doors with a loud sigh. I hate being late and I was about twenty minutes late.

The healer was standing at the front desk with the receptionist waiting for me. As I pushed in the doors she moved towards me, putting her hands up and shushing me. "Woah, shh; so much darkness, so much hate or is it pain... it's okay, you made it." She ushered me into a room. "You can't have kids, you're too uptight. You have three little boys waiting to come to you but they are waiting until you're a little more chilled."

I felt like I had been slapped in the face. So, it was my fault I couldn't have kids. I went into the room a hard, sad, negative ball of hate. I left there, however, with a feeling of drunkenness, relaxed and relieved. Something shifted that night I went there. She knew so much about me and she told me I had a blockage in my ovary left side and that I needed to go and see Eli.

I took myself along to Eli. He had a clinic in Parramatta and the clinic was full of people waiting to see him or to pick up potions. I was a little nervous. So many people to see this old guy… he has got to be good, right? I didn't have to wait long for my appointment. I got called into a second room, more like a consultation room. An assistant went over a few things with me, asked some questions and sat with me. Then Eli walked in, an old white-haired man. I remember he had a bad cough which made me sceptical. How was he going to help me when he couldn't help his own health? Anyway, he didn't say much, looked in my eyes with a light, touched points on my body (sore points), asked me about my blocked left nostril, told me about my digestive system and how it wasn't working well and that my left ovary was sluggish so not ovulating regularly. All this, Eli got from looking in my eyes. I was amazed. He stuck some spray up my nose, which unblocked my left nostril. He told me to cut out dairy for a week and white bread for ever. He gave me a cleanse potion, joint rub and some drops to have every day. As he handed me the drops, he said to be careful as these will make you very fertile and easily to fall pregnant… I couldn't believe it. That's what I was there for, and he did not know that.

I started all my potions the next day. The cleanse was messy and I saw the toilet a lot, but by the end of the first week, it slowed down and I felt so much better. Within the following month, I was pregnant.

I didn't want to tell anyone about this one. I was scared and could only think about how it was going to end with yet another heartache. I was paranoid and anxious. I was in a special high-risk clinic and I was able to get scans regularly to check weekly everything was going okay. At about seven to eight weeks into the pregnancy, I was losing my mind… everything was fine but I couldn't stop the feeling of dread. I phoned up the healer to see if she could help me feel better. I went to her that day. Walking into my appointment and she greeted me with, "Oh congrats on your pregnancy." She knew. In the appointment, she did a mini healing and told me about the future. This was the pregnancy to stay this time and not to stress. Now was the time I was going to be having a boy. It was what I needed to hear. I knew she was right. She said so many other things right about my life, so I knew what she was telling me was to be.

I went on to have my first son, Andrew, in 2009 and I was so elated. I enjoyed my pregnancy and all the things that came along with it. Baby shower, babymoon, doing up his room and fighting over names. As my pregnancy progressed, I couldn't believe it was finally going to happen for us. I was no longer sitting in the empty room that had been set aside for a baby crying and praying to be a mum. Making promises to God that I would be a good mother and I would not be anything like my biological mother. I even wrote up a contract to God with this promise, and I still carry it around in my purse today.

Andrew did come a little early, two weeks after my 30th birthday on the 30th of September. We had been going to Ant's parents for our usual Tuesday night dinner. I stepped out of the passenger seat and my waters broke badly. I remember I screamed and sat down on the driveway. Ant's dad rushed back inside to get me a towel. Ant helped me back into the car and we headed home to get my things. Contractions started in the car and by the time we reached our house (20-minute drive), the contractions were every seven minutes. I crawled around, getting the last of my things together while Ant spoke to the hospital. We arrived at the hospital within ten minutes and the contractions were then five minutes apart. From when my waters broke to when I held Andrew in my arms, it had been 6.5 hours. I had a hard time getting him out and suction, forceps, episiotomy and an epidural is how I got there in the end. Ant's mum had followed us to the hospital and was in the birthing suite the entire time. She was often freaking out, praying a lot, and then crying when they gave me the epidural. It was a little weird for me having my mother-in-law looking up my hoo-ha. I hadn't fully agreed for her to be in there, but because Andrew was early my mum couldn't be at the birth so she saw it as an opportunity to take the free spot.

Again, I was changed. I had everything I had ever wanted. Ant had even stepped up so well in those weeks after Andrew's birth. I had the baby blues pretty bad and I remember feeling overwhelmed with the new experience. Looking back now, I know it was just an adjustment thing and lack of sleep. I felt overly emotional, overly protective and extra judgey of anyone who came near me and my baby.

I disliked my in-laws at this point. I cringed at their stupid culturally dumb opinions and the fact I had to deal with the way they needed to be involved in every bit of my baby's care. My mother-in-law fussed and made me feel inadequate, always telling me how things should be done or making me paranoid because I wasn't doing it a certain way or the way they used to do it back in the 70's. I felt myself being mean but I couldn't stop. Leading up to the birth, Ant's parents had really taken care of everything financially. Ant was working in the takeaway shop waiting to turn it into a café. We had no money. Ant's mum would take me grocery shopping every week and they made sure I had everything for the new baby. So, I knew my attitude towards them was not nice and I really was thankful for all they had done. I think I felt they were encroaching all the time on my bonding time with my baby.

I really just wanted my family around me. Mum and Dad came for a week but it made things worse when they left.

Ant went back to work at the takeaway shop that he was going to turn into a swanky restaurant/cafe in Balmain. So, he was six days a week at the takeaway and those days he worked late into the night also. I was angry. I hated that place. I was left raising a newborn by myself and if I wanted to see my husband more than one day a week, I had to drive me and Andrew into Balmain to see him. Ant had told me before that he was done with the hospitality business, but somehow, we were back here again and I resented that. Working for someone else was never good enough for him. He had a hard time taking direction or instruction from others. He basically hated bosses. Ant always wanted to chase the dollar, with how to make money always at the front of his mind. I think I was disappointed by this. I feel he chose money over his passion and his talent went to waste. I admired his creative and passionate mind and his drive to be more. However, somewhere along the way, his focus shifted to money and he couldn't see the deficit it left in the rest of his life. The way he was raised definitely plays to this also. His dad worked constantly in something he didn't love (chicken farming) and planted the seeds of money being the most important thing in your life. If you have money, everything else will be okay. His dad though, never did anything with them as kids. They hardly ever went on holidays and Ant could never talk to his dad. Today, their relationship is better but his parents can't change their ways, which makes them a prisoner to those ideas and ways.

No matter how much I begged and asked Ant to be around more, he couldn't and wouldn't. His obsession with building his dream restaurant was all he could do and focus on. He had met a new business partner through his coffee repping and she was a chef, a French one at that. To turn the takeaway shop into the French diner Ant and Mellissa (that was her name) had dreamed of, the place needed to be gutted and redone. This would take two years and a heap of legal crap. For those two years, I never saw Ant. Again, always working late, always with Mellissa working through some issue. Yes, I know I should have seen it back then what it really was but I didn't I trusted too much. I went back to dancing, went back to the store part-time and lived the life of a single mum. Sandy and Glen had split and Sandy and I often went away together with Andrew. She was like my wife and an amazing aunty to Andrew.

Ant finally got the diner opened the day I started back at Uni to do my Masters of Education. Andrew started two days of day care and he went to the in-laws for two days a week while I was at uni. Ant and Mellissa were super proud of the diner, and it was doing really well. I just felt I was always waiting for him to be settled and established so he could spend more time with his family. I didn't get a good feeling about Mellissa. I didn't like her much and I couldn't put my finger on it, but I did voice this to Ant before he went into business with her. She was a mother of two kids and had a really nice husband, and we spent a fair bit of time at their place in the planning stage. I was not a fan.

Just before my degree commenced, Sandy, Andrew and I went up to Wonga Beach. Mum and Dad were up there for a bit. We flew up and spent the week camping under the coconut trees. We had a great time. It was there that I realised I was pregnant. I waited until I got home and did a test to see and yes, I was. I had started to bleed a little though, and wasn't overly confident. I had told Ant and we were excited for another bub. I was at work when I started to bleed heavier. I was able to get an appointment at an ultrasound place across the road from work.

I went for my appointment and was told that yes, the baby had died and that I was miscarrying. I went back to work, finished my shift, called Ant and told him what was happening. I went and picked up Andrew and went home. The next day, I had arranged a play date with a mum from playgroup and we were going to Lollypops Playland. Nothing major had happened with the bleeding, so I went to the playdate. It was about an hour into the play date that I felt a massive gush. I also had a massive wave of sickness hit me. I explained to my friend what was happening and I ran off to the bathroom. There was blood everywhere and it had gone through my pad and all over my jeans. I changed, tried to clean myself up, tied a jumper around my waist, had a spew and with shaky legs, walked back out. I met my friend back at the table we were sitting at, every step creating a gush. I explained I needed to go home, and she helped me get Andrew in the car. She was, I remember, concerned for me to drive. I wasn't far from home. Seven minutes in the car and I would be home. I cried the whole way home. Andrew was concerned, asking what was wrong. He fell asleep on the way home and as I got out of the car at home, I was really weak and I couldn't stand up. I sat in the garage in a state of panic. I needed to get Andrew to his bed up three flights of stairs, then he would be safe and I could deal.

I got him out of the car and quietly and very slowly carried him upstairs. Got him into bed and crawled out and down the stairs. The gush wasn't as intense when I crawled. I got down to my phone and called Ant… he didn't answer. I tried a few times, but he still didn't answer. I bled through again and while in the bathroom, I passed out. I came to on the floor of the bathroom. I called Ant again and he answered. I cried and told him what was happening and said I thought I should go to hospital. He was angry and it seemed as though I was annoying him. He didn't think I needed to go to hospital. I hung up and called Jane. I told her what was happening. She said she would come pick me up, take me to emergency, then bring Andrew home to my place and look after him with her daughter. Thank God. She arrived twenty minutes later. I hadn't moved off the lounge since I rang her. She got me into her car and I was sobbing and bleeding badly.

Jane had married a friend of Ant's about two years after we had got married. She and her husband, Damon, lived in Silverdale so she wasn't far. She put Andrew's baby seat in her car and went and woke Andrew up. We sped up to emergency and I got out while she went and parked the car. I shakily staggered in and up to the emergency window. I explained to the nurse at the window what was happening. She took one look at me and took me in to the consult room, then into the emergency room. I had been losing too much blood, so it was an emergency. Jane and the kids found me in an emergency bed. Jane stayed for about half an hour then she left, taking Andrew back to my place. I asked Jane to call Ant when she got back to our place to organise for him to get back ASAP to look after Andrew.

I was in emergency all night and Ant turned up at about 11pm. He hadn't come home early and he came to the hospital to see me. I told him to go home and relieve Jane. They moved me from emergency at some point in the early hours to a bed upstairs. I then had 24 hours of starvation, pain killers, waiting for ultrasounds and then the doctors to approve my DNC. It got late the following day and I was crying constantly, starving and I just wanted to go home. My DNC wasn't going to happen that day because the doctors were in emergencies all day. The nurses told me I could eat dinner and stay overnight to have the procedure the following day. I lost my shit pretty bad and got Ant and Andrew to come and pick me up. I wanted to go home.

I think it was probably two days later, I booked in for the DNC and had it done. Having to relive the entire thing all over again. I remember being emotionally exhausted and crying a lot. I had a really long shower that night, and sat in the bottom of the shower letting the water run over me, hoping the water would wash away my sadness.

CHAPTER 10

Tristan

Life went on, of course. Ant distanced himself as usual and worked a lot. I continued my Masters of Education. I immersed myself in my studies and kept working part-time, and teaching. I had a shaky start to my Masters but once I got into the swing of it though, and remembered how to learn, study and be creative, it was a good distraction and was good for my brain and self-esteem.

It was an 18-month full-time course and into my second year, just after my last practical, I had got casual work at the local high school. I then found out I was pregnant. I was going to be seven months pregnant for my graduation. I have the photos from that day in my gown... yep, looking rather plump. Ant's mum and Jane and Ant came to my graduation. Everyone was super proud and made a big deal. Not Ant though. He, I think, felt a little threatened by my success. It was only when his mum spoke to him about it that he started to make a bit of a fuss about it, bought me jewellery etc. I kept working at the high school up until a week before I had Tristan. I was teaching drama and it was going really well.

Tristan was born on the 4th of March 2013. He was on time and was born in three hours. I woke in the morning at 2am and flew out of bed as I heard my waters pop. I managed to not get it on the bed. We rang Ant's parents, and his dad came to stay with Andrew while we went to the hospital. It all happened rather quickly and by 6am he was in my arms on my chest. He fed straight away and I remember my instant love for him. I was so much more carefree with Tristan. I felt prepared, ready and relaxed. The birth had gone well. So well, in fact, that they wanted to send me home that afternoon. I asked to stay. I wanted one night by myself with my new baby boy. I spent my 24-hour stay relaxing, feeding, having visitors. Andrew came to meet his new baby brother and he was in love. Andrew is sensitive and an old soul, I think. Andrew was calm and happy and a great toddler. He was happy to have a brother.

Tristan was a dream baby and did everything he was supposed to. Ate, slept and hardly cried. He was quiet and seemed a happy baby. My sister, Summa, was having some problems in her life at this time and came to visit to meet her new nephew. She decided to stay with us for a while. She drove back up to Lismore, packed her little car and drove back to Sydney a week later. She was running from a broken relationship and a nothing job. She wanted to study childcare, and didn't have the funds to pay rent and study. So, she enrolled in a Tafe childcare course and lived in our spare room for free. She helped me with the boys when I had to work. It was good to have the company and the help. It also got me out a bit more as we would go out sometimes. Summa stayed with us for about nine months. She completed her course and managed to meet a man from Cairns. When it came to the time we were moving out of our European-style mansion – we had sold it and were moving into a rental for a while – Summa moved to Cairns to be with her man, Craig. The relationship had a shaky ground to start and it still has its moments today, but there is a strong love there. They have one child together, my niece.

Anyway, we sold our house in Glenmore Park. Ant was in the process of selling the diner. We were planning to travel to northern Australia in our caravan. Ant was going through a major court battle with Mellissa. As I had predicted, she was not the nicest of people and she took us for everything. We moved into a rental in Glenmore Park while the case took place and while we waited for the sale of the diner to go through. Finally, in August 2014, everything was sorted. Ant walked away with not much but enough for us to travel for a few months. We had bought a block of land in the Southern

Highlands earlier in the year and we planned to settle out there when we got back from travelling. Mellissa gave Ant a real hard time and the court case really dragged on. Mellissa, I heard from her husband, had left her husband and kids and ran off with a man she met online not long after the case. I really do need to point out here: I told you so!

We packed our Nissan Patrol and caravan and put our stuff into storage. We were ready to hit the road the day after my birthday, 14th of September. We had spent a couple of years planning and talking about it. I had wanted the trip to be a time for us to be us. A time where Ant could only concentrate on being with his family. He didn't handle this idea well and quite early on into the trip, I was doubting he would last. We needed to be back by February 2015, as Andrew was starting Kindy and had been enrolled in a school out in Bargo.

We headed north first as we had a couple of events to attend with my family in Lismore. We took our time heading up there and then hung around up there for a week to attend my brother's wedding (Dylan). We then travelled north, to the Gold Coast, Sunshine Coast, Whitsundays, heading north towards Cairns. Ant was angry a lot and hated the set up and pack up each day. He seemed anxious most of the time and being with us 24/7 was hard for him.

Andrew had his fifth birthday at the Gold Coast. Ant somehow was able to convince me to let him meet up with his cousin and my cousin and go out all night on the Gold Coast, leaving me and the boys in the caravan by ourselves... I just remembered that. Seems a pretty shit thing to do, now I think of it. Andrew and Tristan shared the queen bed down the other end of the van. I had put up a curtain in between them to try and help the settling of Tristan. He had started acting out at sleep time now and it now took hours to settle him and he needed me with him for him to fall asleep. I recall every night on that trip being anxious and upset every bedtime.

We stopped at some great places on the way up to Cairns. I started to feel fat and had got used to drinking beer every afternoon. I started to take runs on the beach and finding places to do workouts. However, I had a big vomit one day and ran to just make it into the caravan's kitchen sink. I stated to Ant, ''It's like I'm pregnant.'' Well, that couldn't be... we had not had sex since my drunken birthday night out before we left and I'd had my period. Anyway, I tried to ignore it. I felt pretty sick though, most days and had lost my energy. I decided that when we got to Cairns and to Summa's, I would do a test to check.

About seven days later, we arrived in Cairns. We set up the caravan in Summa's driveway. It was that first night of being there that I did a pregnancy test. Yep, I was pregnant. Ant was in denial and couldn't believe it, how could it happen? After so many problems having a baby for the first two, now at the worst time, it had happened by accident, even. I had to have a dating scan to see how far along I was. I did that the next day. Nine weeks pregnant and all was going well. I was pretty sick and tired most of the time and the heat of the tropics was not helping. I stopped drinking and started my vitamins. Ant was really scared about another baby. Tristan was getting worse with his sleep patterns and behaviour. We didn't have a home to go home to and we also didn't have a job to go back to. Ant started to try and work out our house plans remotely, trying to get it started so we were not so homeless when we went home.

After Cairns, we packed our car with just camp gear, left the caravan at Summa's and started the journey to Weipa. Mum and Dad, Leon and his new partner (soon-to-be wife), Genea, my nephew, and my brother Jimmy, all lived in Weipa. Mum drove the big mine trucks, Leon the same. He had gone travelling up there initially with his ex (my nephew's mum) and they had stayed to work. His ex ended up getting sprung having it off with multiple men, which was pretty silly really as Weipa is only small and everyone knows each other and one of the guys she got it on with happened to be Leon's friend. Anyway, they broke up.

Leon had met Genea at work while they were both driving the mining trucks and fell in love. She mended his heart and bossed him around enough for him to get his shit together. Leon really is one of the best fathers I know. I mean, besides our own. Anyway, off track... Jimmy (youngest brother) had moved up to Weipa after school and had gotten a diesel mechanic apprenticeship at the mines.

Mum and Dad had followed Jimmy up, him being the baby of the family. He needed help, they felt, so they lived with Jimmy up there. Leon had recently moved in with them also, living in a granny flat under the house. Rent up there is overly priced so it made sense for them to all live together to bring down some of the costs. So that's why we were heading up to Weipa to visit all them, then do Cape York with them.

We started on the road to Weipa and stopped overnight at a roadhouse, and camped out the back of the roadhouse. The road to Weipa has only about three or four places to stop on the way, just roadhouses in the middle of nowhere, places for the trucks to get a feed and fuel and then keep moving. The roadhouse we had camped at overnight had a paddock and a block of toilets out the back, so that's where we stayed. We arrived in Weipa late the next day. We stayed at Mum and Dad's, and we had bedrooms again. It was nice to be in a bed. We had a nice time in Weipa. Dad was our tour guide, taking us here and there.

Then when everyone had their four days off again, we packed the four-wheel drives and started the trip to the Tip. They had all done this trip many times before, and knew all the good spots to swim and see. It was hot, rough and all I felt like eating everyday were hot chips. There were no shops anywhere, though. This part of our trip was the best. It was the only time we got to relax and just enjoy. My family are great campers and they were there to help with the kids and took the stress off me to set up all the time. They all pitched in to get us set up comfortably every day and the kids were entertained too. We saw great places and had great experiences. Ant even enjoyed himself, four-wheel driving, river crossing, not showering, hunting and gathering and late-night drinking around the fire (not me). The very Tip was magical aqua blue water crashing against white rocks. Looking out over the water, you could see little islands dotted off the Tip. The water was so clear and the current is a frenzy up there, moving in all directions, swirling and almost bouncing off the curve of the lands tip and the curves of the islands. The water looks so inviting and beautiful but if crocodiles didn't eat you, sharks would.

We camped back off the beach under the trees at a camp spot my family had been to a few times before. Dad advised us to camp behind the tree line, as crocodiles may come into camp otherwise. We also had to face the doors of our tents away from the water. The kids got so dirty playing in the black sand under the trees. Trying to clean them off at bedtime was a challenge and fresh water was meant to be mainly for drinking and cooking. The next morning, Andrew ran off to play with Leon's son (nephew) before breakfast and Tristan toddled around with them. I started to make coffee on the camp stove and was chatting with Mum.

Ant came out of the tent. "Where are the boys?" he asked.

"They are on the beach with Leon," Mum replied.

I grabbed my coffee and went down to the beach. I could hear the kids all laughing as I walked down the path. When I reached the beach, I almost had a heart attack. There was my brother Leon, standing up to his knees in the water facing out scanning the water. The boys were all naked behind him swimming in the shallows, splashing around, having a great time. Leon had a cake of soap in his hand and was grabbing the boys one at a time, bathing them, all the while scanning the water.

"Holy shit, Leon. What the hell are you doing... the crocodiles!" I cried rather dramatically.

"The kids were dirty, so they are having a bath. Look, Nik, how crystal clear the water is. I could see a crocodile coming from fifty metres away. That's why I'm watching out!" he informed me.

I understood, but I still wanted them out of the water. I went and got the towels and rushed back to the water's edge. I quickly dried them and dressed them. "Don't tell your dad you went swimming just then, okay," I said to them. He would have died at the thought.

We were sad to leave Weipa, especially me. I was sad to be leaving my family. Knowing we were moving on to travel by ourselves again, I was nervous and not trusting of Ant's behaviour. I had another appointment in Cairns, so we went back to Summa's. For a few days, we repacked the van and did washing. It was at this appointment that I found out I was having another boy. To be honest, I was pretty devastated by this news. I really had not wanted to be pregnant, let alone it be another boy. I was not ready for another baby so soon after Tristan, especially with Tristan being so much hard work and taking up so much of my attention. Another boy was going to be more loudness and even less sleep.

Mum and Dad had recently bought a holiday letting house in their beloved Wonga Beach. We were heading up there about one hour north of Cairns. The Wonga house was right on the beach. A white 70's style bungalow house. It sat back from the beach under the tropical trees. It was paradise to us. We moved in by ourselves for a week, then Summa and Craig came up to join us on the weekend. We fished off the beach, swam in the pool and did the tourist thing around the Daintree. The kids loved it there and Tristan was swimming by the time it was time to move on. I had gotten comfortable sleeping in an airconditioned bedroom and being able to spread out. When it was time to go, we were all pretty grumpy. We probably would have been happier to stay there for our whole time but we wanted to see the outback more. We were heading to Uluru.

We left early one morning heading towards Mount Isa. What a long, boring, hot drive... nothing to see for days. I think we took two nights to get to Mount Isa. I don't remember much of the whole trip to Uluru really. I remember we had some car issues, it was super hot, and I was uncomfortable a lot. Ant was angry a lot and I remember we didn't talk much at this stage. We were relieved to get to Uluru, but it was hot. We had three days at Uluru. We strapped Tristan to Ant's back in a hiking kids' carrier and walked the base of Uluru. It really is an amazing sight. The rock formation, the colours and an eerie mysterious vibe to the rock. This was my third time to Uluru, but it was my first time walking the base, which gave a different perspective and with so many more flies to annoy us than when you're above in the wind. We moved onto King's Canyon. Again, it was hot. We only stayed a night out there, walked as much of the canyon as we could and left again. I missed people, I think. We had met people on the way, but it was fleeting and we often moved on a little quick.

Travelling the southern end of the Northern Territory, we started to back track, heading back to Cairns. We had decided to head back to Cairns for Christmas. Everyone (my family) was meeting at Wonga for Christmas. Ant needed to also try and get some things set for our property back home and was finding it hard to make phone calls etc when travelling constantly. I was dying to get back to the comfort of the Wonga house. So, it was about one week out from Christmas when we arrived back to the Wonga house. We were happy to be back in comfort. My family arrived a couple of days before Christmas, and the house was full.

It was a great Christmas. I do remember losing it a bit, though. I was feeling a little trapped, didn't get a break, hot, pregnant, couldn't drink, tired, fat and starting to stress about going home to nothing. Ant hadn't been able to organise anything house-wise and now he informed me we were running out of money.

CHAPTER 11

Leo the Baby Born in the Bush

We stayed around Cairns until the second week of January and then started our journey back south. We arrived back to Sydney ten days later. We went straight to Ant's parents' place. They had just finished building their new home in Brighton-le-Sands. The house was on the Grande Parade, the busiest road in Sydney. I was so depressed. They were happy to see us. They had really been against us going. Now they were under the impression we were going to live with them. We had no house, no money. Andrew could go to the local Brighton school, they kept saying to me. Ant tried to talk me into this also. No way. I was already struggling, knowing I had to be there for the next couple of weeks.

I went out to the property a few times with Ant to talk about what we were going to do. The property had no power, no water and was a full bush block. As the start of school date got closer, Ant tried hard to talk me around into staying at his parents. I refused. He moved the caravan out to the property. A friend went to help him clear a spot and to try and work out solar power, 12 volts, and we got a tank to run on a solar pump. It was a drama and not everything worked. It rained heavily the day before we were going to move out there, and then the lights wouldn't work in the van. Ant and his friend worked at trying to get the caravan liveable off-grid for the next couple of days. The weather was not great. So, the day before Andrew's first day of kindergarten, we booked a motel room out in Picton close to his school. We had two nights there as Andrew had two days of school that week. We then, at the end of his day on Friday, headed back to Ant's parents for the weekend.

For the second week, we stayed in a cabin for a few nights and Ant and I spent the days getting the van ready. I think by the mid-week, we moved back into the van. We had lights and had got a generator to help with the power issue. We had set up the annexe as a second living space. The boys had their toys out there and clothes boxes and our Waeco fridge. It was pretty rough, I have to say, looking back. We had a rubbish pit, which we burned off every week, and we had a toilet in the van which Ant had to empty every few days. We both saved number twos for the morning school drop off, when we would go to the shops after and get a coffee and use the toilet. It was difficult trying to time my pregnant bowels, I have to say. I didn't complain. I had wanted us to be there and at least it was our own space. We had also thought it was only an eight-week thing as our house was being built.

We had gone with a module home through a module homes company. So, the house was started in the factory and it was only going to take eight weeks to build. However, at the time we didn't know the council would be our hold up. The house got delayed and delayed. It got colder and colder and it was not getting any closer to us being in a house. The nights in the van were very draughty and very cold. I went to the local junk shop and Vinnies to get thick blankets to try and insulate the walls of the van. The home company started to see there was a problem and that the council were not going to push our application through in time before baby three arrived. They ended up bringing us a one-bedroom cabin that wasn't being used and put it on our property. It got us out of the dirt, at least, but it was tiny. For the boys, we bought bunk beds and curtained them off in the lounge. We had a bathroom but the toilet only flushed when we had the power on, so the generator was it. We had Foxtel. We couldn't get normal TV, so we had to get Foxtel. We managed, and it was more comfortable than the caravan. We went and got some things out of storage and bought some camp heaters for heating.

I was getting bigger and more anxious. I wanted to feel safe, secure and settled. Ant started a labouring job and I was left alone a bit in the solitude of the bush block and in a new area. I was seeing some counsellors from Community Links to help me settle into the area and give me advice and get me into the community. I was seeing the midwife clinic in Camden. I had taken Tristan to Tresillian for help with his sleep and behaviour. We had a week sleeping at the clinic, so it got me out of the roughness for a bit.

In April 2015, it got really cold, with frost every day and snow just over the mountain from us. Ant had bought an old shipping container so we moved all our things out of storage into the container. It was really hard and took an entire weekend and a hire truck. Our stuff was in Penrith about one-and-a- half hours' away. I was stressing. I wanted all my things for new bub. He needed a bed, some blankets, and I just wanted my stuff. I managed to get some clothes, bassinet, and a breast pump. I put the things in the corner of our small cabin room.

That night was pretty cold. We had got back late after picking up the boys from Ant's parents. We had to drop the hire truck back and I remember we had a hard time scrapping together the fuel money to fill it when we were returning it. The last bit of the 63 dollars, we got it together by using 5 cent pieces from wherever we could find them. It was at this point I knew we were struggling. We actually did not have a dollar. Andrew had school the next day and Tristan was going to start day care. We were highly stressed in everything at this time: how we were living; financially, we were broke; the council was taking forever; and the weather – it was freezing and raining constantly. We were having a hard time getting through the mud on the driveway of the property, getting bogged a few times.

Halfway through April, think I was about 30 weeks pregnant, something woke me. It was a pop, actually, more like a slow pop. I got up and a trickle went down my leg. It wasn't a gush, more like a leak. I sat on the toilet for a bit, and more came again in a trickle. I put a pad on. The trickle was pink in colour, so I knew it was my waters. I woke Ant to tell him. We waited for contractions to start but they didn't really. I got some cramping. I packed some things together, got the boys' school stuff ready. We woke the boys a couple of hours after waiting and it was about 5am at this stage. We got the boys dressed and got in the car to go to Campbelltown Hospital, 35 minutes away. We had phoned ahead to tell them, and luckily a couple of weeks earlier, I had done a mini hospital tour so I knew where to go.

Ant and the boys walked me in. I was a bit scared, and nothing was familiar with this labour. It was too early for him to come and I wasn't prepared enough. The nurses put me in a bed and put a trace on me, then did some examinations. My waters had broken but I had not dilated though. I was not in labour. Ant had to take the boys to school, so he left to take them while I had more tests and ate some breakfast. By the time he returned, I had seen the doctor and had been given a steroid to help baby and another injection to keep him in there for as long as possible. When Ant arrived, the doctor went through everything with him and how I would have to stay in the hospital until the baby is born. The aim was to not have him until the course of steroids for lung development were done.

They moved me to my own room upstairs in the maternity ward and I sent Ant home to organise some things for the hospital. Sandy came to see me and went home later with Ant and the boys to help him with them and Sandy was helping get the baby stuff organised, wash clothes etc. It was so wonderful for Sandy to be there at that time. I was highly stressed about the care of the boys as Ant was not the best at organising or knowing what to do for the boys. She stayed until late that night, then took all the washing home to hers to do.

Ant came back to hospital the next day and hung out for a bit. I was in there for three days, with the same thing every day. Injections and tests, monitors. Every night, I would get contractions and pain. The nurses would give me pain killers every four hours and a tablet to stop labour. On the third night, Sandy, Ant and the boys had visited. Sandy was going to go home to hers and Ant was taking the boys for dinner. I had expressed my concern that I couldn't do another night like the night before and I was sure that bub was going to come out that night. Sandy made Ant promise her he would call her if anything happened and she would come meet him and get the boys. He said he would. They all left and I sat alone in my dark room ready for another annoying, painful, sleepless night.

I slept for a couple of hours and woke to my phone ringing. It was Ant and the boys ringing to say goodnight. They had got bogged in the driveway and the car was stuck up to the doors. Ant had to carry the boys into the cabin. He called our neighbours to bring their tractor to pull the car out. It was pouring, and it all sounded very dramatic. I was very upset by the whole story. I was sobbing, missing my boys and worried. The nurse came in to give me the last dose of steroids and anti-labour drugs. I said good night and hung up. Contractions had started again, so I had some more pain stuff. I got hooked up to the monitor to track the baby. I sat in the dark, crying until about midnight. I calmed down, then had a cup of tea and tried to sleep.

I must have dozed because suddenly it was 2am. I was super uncomfortable. A nurse came in and I told her how uncomfortable I was and that I thought the baby was coming. She said she would get the anti-labour pill as it was probably time for it anyway. She left the room. I rang Ant but he didn't answer. The nurse came back with another nurse and did my obs. They decided to check if I was dilated at all, as I had asked them to a few times already. They didn't believe me when I said I thought the baby was coming. I rang Ant again. The nurse checked me... Yep, six centimetres, I think baby is coming soon. I rang Ant and he answered. I told him the baby was coming soon, to call Sandy and sort out the kids and come. It was close to 3am when I spoke to him... he seemed vague but said okay, he would see me soon.

The pain got worse. I couldn't sit still. I sucked on some gas but it didn't help. At around 3.30-4am, a doctor strolled in to chat... I couldn't chat as I was rolling around in pain. "I want to push!" I screamed at him.

He was still being calm. "You're not ready, I will check you, okay, but you need to lie on your back."

"I can't lie on my fucking back!"

He eventually coaxed me over, then another contraction came and I screamed badly. The doctor tried to widen my knees to take a peek... I remember a massive pain and I felt like a demon possessed. A huge roar left my body. I threw my legs open and a projectile birth liquid sprayed from me.

The doctor had been down there, and he jumped backwards. "Oh, ahh yes, baby is coming, I will get someone."

It's a little blurry after that. A heap of nurses came in and wheeled me to the birthing suite across the hall. I got into the suite. It was cold, I remember that. I pushed twice and he was here. One of the nurses cut the cord and took a photo for me. He was tiny, skinny, but he was crying. They took him straight from me, warmed him up and gave him oxygen. They then took him straight to NIC unit. He was too early, too little and was going to need some help. He was born at 4.15am and he weighed 1.8 kgs. I named him Leo.

I sat in the birthing suite for over an hour alone, wondering what was happening. I really wanted to shower and I was starving. Eventually, a nurse came to get me to take me to my room. They had moved me to a share room, and this stressed me out. As I was collecting myself together, Ant and the boys walked in, looking for me. It was 6am at this time. I had a shower in the birthing suite, then moved to my room. I was pretty upset. My baby wasn't with me and Ant had missed his birth. Ant had gone back to sleep when I had called him, then he got kids ready for school and made his way to the hospital. No urgency at all!

That day in the hospital, I saw many people. Counsellors, NIC unit staff, doctors. They tried to get me to go home if not that day, then it was to be the next day. They didn't have the beds for me to stay. Luckily, the counsellor that had seen me was helping me. She knew my living situation, how it was a little far from hospital. I was leaving my baby at hospital for a minimum of two weeks. I was a mess. I could not leave him. My counsellor knew of the old accommodation out the back of the hospital. It used to be for parents of sick children. It had closed down years ago, but they were slowly refurbishing it to start using it again. They had at this time completed two rooms. It was like a motel room with hospital finishes. It would cost me ten dollars a night. I would get called every feeding time from the NIC unit. So that's what I did. I stayed in there the entire time Leo had to be there. The boys would come visit some afternoons and stay for dinner, then go home. They even stayed one night because there were enough beds for them to stay. It was two weeks later when Leo had put on enough weight, was feeding well and I was comfortable to go. We went to Ant's parents for the first week out, just for warmth, I think.

Once the property dried out a bit, we went home. I can't say I was thrilled to be back in the tiny cabin trying to survive. A few weeks went by with not much progress on the house front. Dad came down to start a few things, to get things a little more comfortable for us. Dad stayed in the caravan while he hooked up our water and set me up a laundry in a little garden shed. He spread recycled concrete on the driveway to stop the bogging. Mum then came down to help too. When they left ten days later, we were more comfortable in our cabin. Power had also been approved to be trenched, so soon we would have power. To pay for power, we sold the caravan and Ant sold his Corvette that had been sitting at his brother's place for nearly two years.

The spot where the caravan sat was now just a fenced area of nothing, so it was our dog yard. Penny and Boo lived in there. It stopped them from wandering away all the time. Boo was our bulldog. Ant had bought her when I had miscarried many years before, and she was a great dog. Boo and Penny got along nicely and did everything together. My animals are very important to me and I have always loved animals. I was just thinking about the importance of animals in my life the other day. I'm always looking for or wanting more animals. I find them to be a comfort. I found myself wondering why this was, just two days ago when I was out feeding and talking to my chickens. And the sadness I feel when my alpacas won't let me hug them. I feel as though my love of animals came from my childhood when I was alone, or left alone. We always had dogs and I remember sleeping under the house with the puppies, carrying puppies around all the time. I also ran away once and walked to the outskirts of Mount Molloy and my dog, Tasha, came with me. I have always had animals and so my adult life is no different. Anyway, that was just a thought I wanted to throw in that came to me.

The house slowly was being completed and Ant kept harassing the council. By September that year, 2015, it was approved. The house arrived in five pieces in early November, with a giant crane lifting the pieces into place like a puzzle. Then two days after it had arrived, the builders stuck it together, and finished off the details internally. We were in. We were so happy. Our house was small but we were so excited to be out of the cabin and we all had our own room. We could finally start to settle into our life. It had been hard for so long that I had kind of forgotten how to be happy and how to enjoy life. We had been just trying to survive. I felt lonely, sad and quite disconnected from everything. I had been allocated a lady, Lynne, who would come once a week to help, talk, have coffee etc. She was wonderful. Once a week, she would visit or get me to meet her somewhere local for coffee or a walk. Lynne was a local for over 30 years and she knew everyone and everything. She got me out of the house and helped me gain my social confidence back. She introduced me to the local gym in Picton. She worked there as a child minder, so she knew I could go to the gym and leave Leo with her in the creche. Starting at that gym in late 2015 was the best thing I ever did. I met my group of girlfriends there and we have been tight ever since.

I also joined the local soccer club. I used to play back in the city days and loved it. This soccer club was classified as Southern Highlands, which meant we got to head south for games some weekends. We would head off in the car, all rugged up, doing almost like a tourist drive every Sunday. Ant wasn't a fan of me playing, as it meant he had to look after the kids when I played. However, I felt I was joining my community and I got to socialise, not just be a mum 24/7. I wasn't too bad at it either, and I used to have so much fun.

Back to the gym. Leo and I would go most mornings and the days Tristan wasn't in preschool, he would come too. I had made some friends and we often went for coffee after our class. The friends I had were similar to me – mums that were trying to reconnect with a life. I was able to talk out my issues with them and we became very close. Leo's first birthday rolled around and we were having his circus-themed party at the sports club. I invited some of my new friends and invited a real new one, Nicole. I had only started talking to her a couple of weeks before, and last minute had told her to bring her two kids down to the party on the weekend. She did and she was my kind of person. We clicked instantly. She radiated nice and fun. We had a lot in common and from then on, we have remained close. She is the most reliable, supportive person I know, besides Sandy, of course.

Through my soccer club, I was able to suss out a teaching job through one of the girls in my team. She passed on my resume to the school she was temping at and that was how I got back into teaching, just casual about three days a week at a school in Mount Annan, 30 minutes away. I would drop the kids every morning, well three days, to school, day-care and then continue to work. It felt good to be contributing to finances again. I had my own money.

Things in 2016 were going along rather pleasantly. We hardly saw Ant again. He was on a new money-making venture and had opened a new shop, a pizza shop. He was going large and going to franchise and expand the brand. I plugged away at work, and looking after the kids, going to the gym when I could and soccer on the weekends. The kids were doing gymnastics and loving it, but Tristans's behaviour was a constant issue. He was not sleeping properly, was having meltdowns a lot and just generally not listening. I had taken Tristan and Leo to Karitane for sleep school again. Leo was still waking for a bottle through the night, so thought I would get help for both of them. During our stay this time, Tristan and I did a few behaviour and parenting workshops. I left after the four days feeling like a failure of a parent as I had not been parenting properly. The clinic had enrolled us into an ongoing program which was once a week for six months, called PPP (Positive Parenting Practices).

Tristan and I would go every Friday to the clinic, and Leo would go to Nicole's to hang. The clinic involved us sitting in a room playing with toys. I would wear an earpiece and a nurse would sit and watch the play, prompting me to praise or speak to Tristan. We worked on timeout, quiet chair and other not-so-positive situations. I hated the clinic. It made me feel like the worst parent in the world. Some of the practices would work for a bit, but then would become ineffective again. When we reached our six-month mark of the program, the nurse spoke to me about Tristan's progress and how he really wasn't making a major improvement. She had spoken to the clinic psychologist who had looked in on some of our sessions, and the psychologist seemed to believe there was an underlining issue with Tristan.

We got sent off to do different tests and to see a paediatrician. He had a hearing test to see if that was an issue. Nope, he had super hearing so that couldn't be an issue. The paediatrician had a long wait list and it took about five months before we got to see him. We had been still going to the clinic every fortnight and the psychologist (Mary) had taken to our case and was helping to navigate me and Tristan to get help. She was under the impression that he had ADHD. She had a son with it and Tristan, to her, was showing signs of it. She worked with me on strategies for handling his behaviour, sorted him with sensory toys and kept me educated on the ins and outs of ADHD. Mary helped me get my papers together for getting Tristan tested and helped me with my reports and what I needed to say to the paediatrician to get him prioritised. So, by the time we got into see the paediatrician, we were ready and educated. I was not upset any more with worry about what was wrong with him. We went into the appointment two hours late. The doctor was running behind, as he often does. I handed him Tristan's file and we discussed behaviours, issues, lack of sleep, and who we had been seeing. The paediatrician wasn't overly talkative and he wasn't overly concerned. Tristan sat in the corner of the room, quietly playing a puzzle. The doctor said he would put him on the list with the CATS team but it was about an 18-month wait. He started to talk about Tristan being my first child and not having anything to compare his behaviour to.

"Ahh no, he is my second child and he has two brothers," I said to him.

At this point, his attitude to me changed. He listened more, watched closely. It seems he had thought I was being an overreactive first-time mum. This changed everything. He did the referral letter then and there, and sent Tristan for a blood test to check there wasn't anything health-related. We booked in for another appointment in three months' time and I had a list of tasks I had to do before that next visit.

Tristan had his college visit day at the same school Andrew was attending. He got dropped off in the morning and I picked him up a few hours later. I had been worried about sending him, as I was worried that his behaviour would result in him not being able to go to the school. When I picked him up, his teacher hadn't said anything negative about his day, so I thought yes, he held it together for the day. Tristan had been behaving badly at preschool and was spending some of his days sitting in the office, so I was concerned.

A week after Tristan's paediatrician appointment and a few days after his college day, I was driving to pick the boys up from preschool, afterschool care and day-care, when the paediatrician called me. "Tristan's blood tests have returned and I'm sorry to tell you but he has high indicators of coeliac disease." He was going to get his friend, who was a paediatric stomach doctor, to call me. I sat in the carpark at the preschool, discussing with the stomach doc for about half an hour. Tristan was going to go and have to have an endoscopy to confirm the diagnosis.

About two weeks after that conversation, we travelled to Double Bay Day Surgery and had his case confirmed. I did a lot of research and started collecting gluten-free recipes. We gave Tristan a week of free-for-all eating anything he wanted, as his last goodbye to his favourite gluten-filled foods. It was a massive shift for the family and we tried to all eat gluten-free. However, we have now settled into Tristan having his own food and we all eat gluten-free dinners. The same day that I received the phone call about him having coeliac disease, I also got a phone call from the college about Tristan's college day the week before. It was the school's psychologist. She was ringing to chat about his behaviour on the day and how it was a concern. He had not participated, had yelled and been pushy with kids wanting to be his friend, and he wouldn't follow instructions. I listened and asked why I wasn't told this when I picked him up on the day. The conversation was heading down the path of them not wanting him to come to the school. At this stage, I was getting emotional. I was feeling sorry for Tristan. My poor little boy was not going to be able to eat gluten ever again and now this bitch was telling me he wasn't normal and that he was not going to fit in. I told her everything I knew so far about Tristan and his issues, and how we were waiting for an assessment and we believed he had ADHD. I felt like I was betraying him by telling them, like it was a secret and now he would be worse off and singled out.

The school was actually the opposite. It was probably the best thing I could have done. The way they saw it was that I was trying my best to get him help and now that they knew this, they would be able to work with me. Tristan got his offer into the college for transition for 2017. He was excited to be going to the same school as his big brother Andrew.

At the end of 2016, Tristan had his assessment 11 months after joining the waitlist. It was a full-day assessment by a panel of experts. He went through a range of physical and cognitive tests, along with some intense questions. At the end of the day, they called us into a consult room. They ran through the results of the tests they had conducted and then concluded Tristan had autism. They said that they were very sorry. I cried a lot… I wasn't ready for that one. I knew ADHD inside out, but I didn't know anything about autism. I mourned for my son that day. He would have this forever. How would he go through life and be normal? I of course know now that this was not a grim sentence for him but at that time, I was scared of the road ahead.

I was scared to tell Ant. He hadn't exactly been supportive in my findings of Tristan's conditions. He always put it down to Tristan's behaviour being just a boy thing and that he was maybe just a little asshole. Ant had never come to an appointment and when I had given him information about it, he never read it. Everything was BULLSHIT to him. So, I prepared myself with the report and gave it to him that night. He didn't say much, just said something about a second opinion. I explained to him it was a panel that had given this diagnosis, not a single doctor. We argued about it for a bit and Ant left the conversation with his usual dismissive and annoyed behaviour.

CHAPTER 12

Marly, my Marvellous Mistake

For Christmas 2016, we went to Cairns. All the family booked cabins at Wonga Beach (we couldn't use the holiday house as it was booked). We flew up, hired a car and drove to Wonga. We had Christmas together, with Mum and Dad, Summa and Craig, Leon and Genea, Dylan and his son, Jimmy and us. Ant ended up flying back on boxing day to go back to work and I stayed with the kids. Mum and Dad helped me a lot, but I remember how hard I was finding it, I was exhausted, I think. Leo wasn't sleeping properly, and Tristan was misbehaving a lot. Tensions were high with Ant and I — I was at the point of not wanting to be with Ant anymore. He didn't listen to me, made me feel like I was doing things wrong all the time, and expected me to always look after the kids. We had no romance anymore. We hardly spoke and he was stressed by the kids all the time. We were forever walking on eggshells around him, when he was around, that was. He was generally just mean.

After Christmas, we moved into the Wonga house for a week, with everyone. All the cousins got to play and bond. It was nice times. I remember Leon getting up at night to help one of my crying kids. He would pass me in the hall and we would nod, shrug, roll eyes and keep moving. After Wonga, we had a few days in Cairns CBD in a nice hotel, with Leon and Genea and kids, they had just had another baby boy. Ant flew up to meet us again and stay a few days to fly back with me. We still weren't getting along. I was highly stressed and angry, and sad all the same time. He was pestering me for sex the entire time we were there and this caused more fights when I wouldn't. It was on our last night before we flew home that I gave in and had sex with him. We weren't using protection. He assured me he would pull out in time. He didn't. I believe I hit him and yelled a lot about it. It was soon forgotten though, and life settled back into life.

I missed a period. I knew I was pregnant. It was only missed by a few days but I thought it would just be our luck. I didn't say anything to Ant. He wasn't around much anyway. I did a test and yep, I was. I took the kids to school, and went to the gym. Most of the girls were there sitting on the floor, waiting for the class to start, talking crap as usual. I put my bag down, stood in the congregation.

"So, guess what happened to me?" I announced.

One of the girls looked up at me laughing, "You're pregnant." All the girls had a giggle.

"Yep."

OH MY GOD. Their reaction was shock and disbelief. They all knew the problems I was having with Tristan and Leo wasn't great either (hard work) and now I was going to have another baby. They were a little confused at my being able to do that, as in, get pregnant, when I was not on the best terms with Ant. They wanted to know how Ant reacted. I filled them in on how I hadn't informed him yet!

On the way home, I stopped into Nicole's. I hadn't told her yet as she hadn't been at the gym that morning. I told her. She laughed and cried because I had started crying… not tears of happiness. I was scared that my mental health wasn't going to cope with number four. It had only been two weeks before that I had hit rock bottom. I had a breakdown. I almost drove away one night and left the kids. Andrew chased me down the driveway and I stopped. I was hysterical. Andrew ended up calling Ant. He came home eventually. I was in a ball on the floor, sobbing and uncontrollable. The next morning, I think Ant got the kids to school and I got up and went to the doctor. I was prescribed anti-depressants and given a referral for a marriage counsellor and a psychologist. I started my pills that night and by the time I had found out about pregnancy number four,

I was mentally feeling more stable. Actually, I couldn't believe I had let myself feel that shit for so long. The pills helped me see things so much clearer and I was able to make better decisions. I started to feel more confident and could articulate my thoughts.

So, Nicole's reaction was a lot like everyone else's first reaction to the news. Happy, but concerned for me. Ant's reaction was not so happy. He did not want another. We didn't have room and how would I cope? I assured him he probably wouldn't be involved much, just like usual, and I would cope with the help of my pills, and our babysitter, Georgina, would be there to help. I was confident I was having a girl this time... I had always been told by clairvoyants that I was going to have a girl. This time it had to be my girl. So as soon as I could find out the sex via the genetic blood test, I found out it was a girl. She was due in September, actually on Andrew's birthday.

I was calm, and enjoyed my pregnancy this time round, knowing this was my last. I got a little sick and experienced general discomfort, but I still went to the gym and work. I did develop really bad carpal tunnel syndrome, which didn't go away after birth either. I had to get corrective surgery to fix it eventually. I think I worked out that I had not slept on my side or any other way besides propped up with my arms over pillows on my back for about 2 years. From the start of pregnancy until my surgery, it was two years of constant pain, numbness and hardly any sleep. As soon as I had the surgery, it was instantly better. I went away with the girls two days after surgery. I wasn't able to even dress myself, and my hands were bound up in claws. Nicole had to shower me. Bit funny.

We were getting an extra bit made for the house through the same home company that built the first part. We were adding two extra rooms and a rumpus area. Leo's room was going to be the hall extension and office. We were trying to rush it through before our baby girl arrived. Ant and I had started to see a marriage counsellor, much to Ant's disgust. He had agreed because I wasn't able to keep going with how we were running and had explained that to him. So, he agreed and we saw someone every two weeks. I was happy the guy was definitely on my side and called Ant out on a lot of his bullshit. The kids got minded by the sitter and we would often go out for dinner after our appointment. We were doing better once Ant stopped taking the piss of the counselling. He had a little emotional breakdown in one of the sessions and ended up in tears. From then, we were happier in our relationship. A wall had come down and I think he realised what kind of husband he had been.

I had been going to Bowral antenatal clinic and had been seeing a psychologist through the hospital. Her name was Lucy. I talked out my everyday with her: the kids, Ant and my feelings about the pregnancy. She often gave me things to work on and think about, but mostly she made me think about me and what my wants were. She built me up every session and I felt empowered every time I left her sessions. With Lucy backing me, I wanted to do more, be more. I finally felt in control of my life again. I wanted to be her friend. Every woman/mum needs a Lucy. Towards the end of my time with Lucy, she had asked me to think more about what I wanted in life, and what I wanted for me.

This was the point where Shooting Stars was born. I decided I wanted to open a dance school. I wanted to go back to dancing and build a business. I chattered excitedly with Ant about my vision and I was going to give myself two years to get it going. Ant was very negative about it, talking about set-up costs and what was going to happen to the kids while I was trying to get a business going. I talked it out with Jane, Nicole and Sandy. I also talked it out with Mum and Dad. If it hadn't been for Lucy though, Ant's negative remarks may have stopped my dream.

The extension of the house arrived early September, and some of my girlfriends helped me pack up Tristan's and Andrew's rooms and move them to the other end. We set up a lounge room with all the overflow toys and books in it. I had a couple of false alarms with the pregnancy, thought my waters broke once when it was me pissing myself because I had been yelling at Leo so badly. One night, I thought I was in labour. We went to the hospital, only to have to go home an hour later. Our neighbour got dragged out of bed to watch the kids at 2am.

Sandy had lost her job, which was lucky for me, because in the first week of September when we were moving stuff into the other end and setting up the baby's room, Sandy had time to come stay out at our place. Ant was working late every night and I was worried he wouldn't make it back in time. So, Sandy came out to hang for a few days and nights. She was due to go home the day we finished the nursery. Ant came home in the afternoon and insisted she stay one more night so they could have a drink and a catch up. I was feeling pretty yuck and sore by this point. I had helped move things around. I was happy for her to stay again to help. I went to bed fairly early that night, 9.30ish, I think. Sandy and Ant were just going to have one scotch and go to bed also. Sandy was sleeping in the baby's room on a mattress.

I got up at about 3am needing to wee and my waters broke. I went in to tell Ant, got my hospital bag and baby's bag, and put on some clean pants. Pain started mildly but it was definitely there. I went in to Sandy to tell her we were going to hospital and my waters had broken. She was staying with the kids. Thank God she had stayed that extra night. We drove to Bowral. Ant drove fast because we were nervous about having baby in the car. We got to the afterhours entry and a nurse met me at the doors with a wheelchair. Everyone on the staff knew me from my false alarms and I had been on watch with the worry the baby would come too early. I had been holding on from 35 weeks. Bowral Hospital, being a country town hospital, would not let me give birth there under 36 weeks. Also, a week before, a lady with her fourth pregnancy gave birth in the carpark, so everyone was ready for me to go quickly. I was now in labour. I had made it to 36 weeks and 4 days.

The hospital was really quiet. I got into the birthing suite and contractions increased. I sucked on some gas, walked around a bit, and tried to vomit. Ant tried to sleep and occasionally cracked a stupid joke. We had the one midwife and she was great. When it came time to get baby out, I was on my knees hunched over the back of the bed. The midwife told Ant to get ready to deliver the baby. He was shocked and looked apprehensive. I screamed and pushed a couple of times and in a loud deep roar I pushed, and out came Marly. Ant caught her underneath me and cut the cord. She was tiny and beautiful. She cried and was born at 5.45 in the morning on 9th of

September 2017. She was cleaned off with a warm towel and placed on my chest. I was so happy to have my little girl.

I had a shower in the birthing suite and then we were moved to a room in time for breakfast. Marly slept quietly beside me the entire time. Ant decided to go home. I decided that I was going to stay at the hospital for a minimum of three nights. I wanted the bonding time, the peace and quiet. After two days, we had some routine test done so we could get ready to go home. The nurse mentioned Marly was looking a little jaundiced and that she would need to go into the blue lights overnight. That wasn't concerning for me. All but Tristan had had some level of jaundice.

After overnight with the blue lights, Marly had her heel pricked again. We had to wait a while for the results. Her jaundice was not coming down. If anything, it had increased. The on-staff paediatrician had a talk to me about having to stay longer and Marly would have to go into a humidicrib under the lights for another 24 hours with regular feeds, possibly feeds from a bottle to get it to flush her system quicker. I was packed and ready to go home that day. It was the day before my birthday and I was worried about the boys. When they told me I had to stay, they said I could go home for a few hours see the boys and to leave a feed with them for Marly when she woke again. My friend, Em, had come to visit me at the hospital and she said she would give me a lift home.

I went home for a few hours, got some more bits and pieces, did some washing, did some cleaning, and organised dinner for the boys. Then when Ant got home and Georgina the sitter arrived, Ant drove me back to the hospital. Marly and I were to have an extended stay at the hospital. Her levels kept rising and it got to the two-week mark before we were able to go home. We got to go home a night here and there but always had to go back for blood tests next morning, then we would be back in overnight because her levels had risen again. Dad had come for a few days to help at home and then Mum came and took over. It was during Mum's visit we were eventually able to go home for good.

Marly was a perfect baby, slept well, fed well and was a happy baby. Everyone that meets her loves her, even today. Clairvoyants had told me a little girl was going to be sent to me, to save my sanity. I strongly believe this, as she instantly makes me feel better and she knows when I'm upset. She is always trying to help and she bosses her brothers around really well. She is calming for Tristan and entertains Leo. Andrew would do anything for her and Ant is smitten with her.

CHAPTER 13

Antonio Lost

Life settled into a routine after Marly was born. The boys went to school and appointments, did their gymnastics. I continued going to the gym and seeing my friends. I felt I was coping with things okay. I started thinking more seriously about my dance school and started researching the hows and what I was going to do. Nicole had taught tap in the past, so she was going to be my tap teacher. She was also good with admin, so I would talk things out with her a bit. In June of 2018, I went to the Gold Coast for a dance convention through the Australian Teachers of Dancing that I had become a member with, for my dance school. I went by myself for two days. I learnt a lot and my confidence grew about my idea. The convention was for studio owners and it helped me grasp the idea that I could do it.

Ant had at this stage lost his pizza chain. It had collapsed and a heap of money was owed. He slipped into a really dark place. He hated everyone, was awful to be around and the kids feared him and his moods. I could not talk to him about anything, especially my dance school. As the months of 2018 ticked by, Ant got worse. We had no money. I ended up going back to work at the local high school to help out. There were things that I needed to buy to start my business that I just couldn't afford. Ant stated rather meanly that he had nothing to give me to help. He even told me I was being selfish thinking about starting a business now. I was wanting to open in 2019.

Ant was having a hard time trying to recover mentally from the fall-out of the pizza shop collapse. I really didn't give him the time. I was upfront when he first started the idea with his dodgy friend. I asked him not to do it. I wanted him to get a normal job and work at that, or I even suggested he do a little café locally if he really needed to get back into the industry. He talked his way around me, like the other times, promising great things and that after a bit of long hours, it would settle into more of a run-itself enterprise. I knew he was never going to listen to me, so I just shut off, didn't want to know about it, didn't ask about it and I guess minded my own business, concentrated on the kids and raising them.

We were fighting a lot and a day before Andrew's birthday we had a massive fight. Ant swore a lot, threw things and said he wanted a divorce. He left the house in a storm and didn't return until early the next morning. We were taking the kids to the snow for Andrew's birthday, staying overnight along the way. I had got up that morning, thinking I was going to go by myself. However, Ant got ready that morning, and slumped into the passenger seat of the car with the intention of coming.

We didn't talk for hours. I felt sick. I even pulled over at one point in the journey to vomit, crying and driving the entire way. Ant was angry at me and I remember the hate in his voice, telling me to shut up. I tried to talk about it, and ask him about what he'd said. He was spiteful, but said he didn't actually want a divorce, he was just mad. He had nothing more to say about it. We got to the snow fields. It was the last day of the season and we got to toboggin and play in the snow for the afternoon for free. The kids had a wonderful time but Ant was awful the entire day, and I felt it was no longer salvageable, that our family was definitely breaking up after this.

Ant tried to pretend things were normal for the next couple of months. He hid from most people. People and sheriffs were coming to the house to get money. He put his head in the sand, deep into his depression, and the debt got worse. I was sick of the emotional and financial abuse and I reached out to his brother. Something needed to be done. He needed medication.

One Sunday, under the pretence of his brother's birthday, we went to his Mum and Dad's (they now knew about his depression too). We had lunch, discussed life. Ant pretended he was normal. Then his brother (a pharmacist) presented him with a box of antidepressants. Ant made some joke and tried to hand them back. His dad walked over to him and told him he had to take them, and his brother said he needed them.

Ant said, "Oh, is this an intervention? Haha." He looked over at me.

"Yes, it is. You need to take these or you can't come home," I replied in a shaky voice.

He was mad but could tell the seriousness of it. He took his first pill there in front of us. We got in the car and drove home in silence. I made him an appointment for the doctor the next day and wrote him a list as to what he needed. A psychologist referral, to check his medication dose and generally get help. He went, started a proper dose, and saw a psychologist a couple of times. He didn't like the shrink, and the medication made him sleepy. He stopped seeing the shrink and stopped his meds. He had shown a calmer side when he was on them, but he felt they didn't really work. The shrink had diagnosed him with a multiple personality disorder and bipolar, so he didn't like her.

We went on like this for the rest of 2018. I borrowed money from Sandy to buy my dance stuff. I couldn't get a space to rent, so I was going mobile. I needed to buy the teaching syllabus, register the business, get some posters and flyers printed, and I needed a portable ballet barre and I had ordered some uniforms which I hadn't paid for yet. Sandy gave me $5000 to get those things, and it was the only way I could get started. Our friend did all my logo stuff and he even tried to make my portable mirrors. As the new year started to get closer, Ant sourced me an old car with a tow ball, and a friend gave me a trailer (we paid him for it). Dad came down in early January to paint my trailer the dance school colours. I had secured a pay-by-the-week church hall in Picton. I would be setting up and packing up every day. I was being stubborn. I had something to prove now and I didn't want to give up. Mum and Dad didn't have the money to give me, so I was so grateful Sandy offered to lend me the money so I could follow through with my dream. We decided to not tell Ant that it was her that lent me the money. She said just tell him it was your parents. He would accept that better than money coming from her.

So that's what I did... he actually didn't even query it for a couple of months until I think when I asked him about the ballet barre arriving by courier. I asked if had arrived that day. He said yes, it did, and how did I afford it? That's how I came to follow through with our little white lie. "Yeah, Mum and Dad gave me the money." I had never lied to Ant before, but here I am, living the lie well until now, until he reads this. He has lied to me many times, so I think I can get a little one in there.

For New Year 2019 we went to Copeton Dam. We had not been back to Copeton since Pop had died. The entire myside of the family used to go out there every year for about ten years. We would camp on the water's edge, water ski, fish and drink a lot. We used to have the best time. Anyway, since Mum and Dad had returned to Lismore and weren't living so far away, we were going back this year. It's about a seven-hour drive for us from Sydney. We packed my trailer with camp gear and the dogs, and left. The drive seemed to take forever, traffic was full-on and Ant's anxiety was through the roof. He slept a lot along the way and yelled at the kids a lot. We arrived late that afternoon at Copeton and then had the struggle of setting up the camp. It was very windy. All my siblings were there with their kids and families. Dad walked up the hill where we decided to set up camp. He came up to help. It took a bit of time and when we were set, it was dark.

Usually at meal times we would all meet in the communal area and eat and drink for hours. Ant would not leave the back of our car. He had skulled half a bottle of scotch and was not wanting to talk to anyone. He didn't even say hello to most of my family. He used the kids as an excuse to stay at the camp. I went up to put them to bed and he said he would stay and watch them. My sister and brother, Dad, sister-in-law all went up to chat to him and try and get him to come join us but he wouldn't. Ant remained this way the entire week we were there. On our last day, we were all sitting by the water and everyone had been skiing. I had been trying to get Ant to have a go the entire week. He finally gave in and got ready with skis on and in the water. Dad was driving the boat. Ant had skied in the past and he stood up straight away. He looked pleased with himself. The boat had got about 500m from the shore when he came off. It didn't look like he hit hard. There was kind of slack in the rope and he sunk. However, the bloodcurdling scream and swearing that he went on with would prove otherwise.

Dad circled back to Ant and stopped next to him, trying to pull him in the boat... he kept screaming. All we could see from the shore next was Dad jumping in the water to save him. Next, my brother, Jimmy, and Summa's partner, Craig, dived in from shore and swam out to help. Jimmy and Craig swam Ant back in and he lay on the mud bank shaking, groaning, swearing. Mum checked his leg out. He had snapped something muscular. Dad and my brother loaded him onto a surfboard and put him into the back of the car. Mum gave him a hardcore painkiller and he seemed to not be so worked up anymore. Dad drove him into the hospital and they were gone for most of the day. When they returned, Dad backed the car up to the camp and opened the back doors of the car so he could still be part of the group. Ant was pretty out of it up to eyeballs in pain meds so he was in out of consciousness. We put him on an air mattress and chucked a blanket over him. He had torn a muscle off something in his leg/thigh and it was swollen and blue. At the end of that night, we closed the back of the car and left him to sleep. I went up to my tent and slept, wondering how I was going to pack up and then drive all the way home the next day. It was quite the ordeal trying to pack up. Mum and Dad were trying to help look after the kids and feed the kids while trying to pack the trailer. It really was a trip from hell on the way home. Ant slept most of the way and we arrived home quite late that night.

Ant's mental health got worse after his accident, and he was hating life a lot at the time. I was getting into promo mode for my dance school and preparing for the registration day we were having that weekend. I was excited and nervous at the same time. I was worried that it would fail and I wouldn't get any students and then

Ant would be right. Our registration day was okay. I had ten students sign up that day, and then the following weekend another five signed up when I did a promo day at the local shops.

Shooting Stars Dance Academy opened its doors (well, church hall doors) in 2019 the first week of February. I had 15 students enrolled and I was inspired. I didn't make any money, but I was able to pay Nicole for the classes she did and Ally, who was my acro teacher. With the help of my casual teaching at school, I was also able to cover my rent. Through the first two terms, I was able to get a few more students. By term three, we moved to a rented space within a self-storage facility. Ant actually helped me. He negotiated for the two units side-by-side and then got his building friend to help put in floors and the wall-to-wall wardrobe with mirrors. It was a little rugged, but it was my own space now and even the students felt proud.

Ant kind of floundered his way around for most of the first half of the year. Then in July/August, he got a job with a delivering company. He hated it but it got him out of the house and gave him a bit more of a purpose. We had another intervention with him at some point and he did go back on his medication and started seeing a psychologist again. He was doing better.

It was back at the beginning of the book where I described my pain over my abortion. This took place in the first term of me opening my dance school. Early days and I couldn't even have my breakdown properly. It was the first week of the holidays, about two weeks after the trauma. That's about the only way I could describe it. Trauma. I did lose it. Leo had been diagnosed with ADHD and ODD and his behaviour was just embarrassing. Put Tristan and Leo together, and life was impossible. Ant was not supportive, very selfish in his own shit and I never had a moment of rest. The trauma caught up to me and I broke down. I went back to the doctor to up my medication dose. Then, within a couple of weeks and back to dancing, I was feeling better and coping again. This though, is how it always feels for me, that I'm always just coping or that I'm not coping. Can't it just be easy sometimes?

Nobody really wants to go through life just coping. Windows of happy times are very far and few between. Sometimes, I amaze myself that I get up and keep going every day. I feel guilty for not being a calm and happy mum. I feel guilty for allowing Ant to be how he is. I feel like his mental state is enabled by me. I enable him to be how he wants to be and I'm not strong enough to stop it. He knows he can manipulate me and my emotions and I will accept his lies and his fake façade. I'm guilty of not pulling him up enough on his behaviour to the kids, and often I'm asking myself why, why am I a stupid woman who allows it? Always thinking things will get better, that he will snap out of it soon enough, that he will want to be a better person, a better husband and a happy father. So, I keep holding on... is it because of this that I don't deserve to be loved and I don't deserve to be happy?

Woah, that was a little woe-is-me moment, sorry. These are just thoughts that I often have and I'm trying to process them and make sense of them, I guess. Anyway, moving on.

CHAPTER 14

Reaching and Shooting Stars

Of course, 2019 did not get easier. My only sanity was my dancing and my outlet. I was able to cater my school for those that couldn't usually afford to do dancing, as I offered payment plans. Of course, people took advantage and I always had to chase money. I let all students be part of performance troupe and we were able to do some eisteddfods, even. We didn't win but did okay for first-time dancers. The studio kept me busy and by the end of 2019, I felt my dream had come true. All I wanted for 2020 was to make some money.

Through dancing, I had become involved in my community and was feeling happy and accepted. I started some therapies for the boys and was finally getting help with payment through the NDIS. Marly was happy and well-adjusted to the chaos of our loud house. Andrew had been doing well at school and dancing at SSDA, loving hip hop. The end of 2019 was winding up on a positive, really. We were losing our babysitter, Georgina. She was moving to the city to have a life or something. So, we had to find a replacement, and that's how we ended up with Reanne. She answered my ad, my plea for help. I had interviewed a few that hadn't worked out and it was getting close to the end of the year. She came for a trial and pretty much didn't leave. Georgina took Reanne through the routine a few times and she was ready.

After the dance concert was a success, I felt like I wanted to celebrate. I had made it through my first year of business, had made some new friends and my reputation as a nice person was intact. I had made it through Ant's constant shit and my kids were alive and relatively happy. Ant and I had another fallout from his business crap, which had come in the form of an accountant. She had been working with Ant in the pizza business (he had known her from school). Anyway, she started displaying obsessive behaviours towards Ant and was stalking him, really. She turned up at our house one night at 2am, drunk off her head, going on. She came into my room. It was scary. I had accused Ant of having an affair with her then, but apparently not. She was tied up in the business and when things started to go badly, she was freaking out. Even after there was no business anymore, she tracked Ant down and knew what he was up to all the time. She would call and hang up. She hacked Ant's Facebook and knew all his contacts.

One day, I can't remember the date, but it was in November just before our concert. I was about to leave home for the studio, when I got a phone call… it was a lady telling me Ant was in a motel with Hayley (someone else he used to work with). The person kept repeating it and saying they were at this certain motel and I should check it out. I hung up, very shaky, and had that sick feeling wash over me. I tried to call Ant but his phone was off. I was getting really worked up, and I rang Nicole. I told her what had happened. She hung up from me and rang the motel. Reanne turned up at my place to do the afternoon shift with the kids and saw my hysteria. She jumped on the phone to her friend who lived near the motel, and told him to drive by and see if Ant's car was there. Nicole couldn't get any info out of the motel manager and now she was crying for me.

I had to go to my studio, so I left and arrived at dancing to a message on my phone from Reanne. Her friend had seen Ant's car at the motel. I tried multiple times to call Ant. Nicole came to the studio to help me get through my classes. I only had the teens that afternoon, so they were pretty supportive. This saga seemed to drag on for hours, and it wasn't until I was picking up the boys from gymnastics after 7pm that Ant rang me. I had left him messages telling him I knew, that he was disgusting and that he was not to come home and I was going to call the police. He was confused and didn't get it or why I was going on like this. I eventually told him what had happened and how it was proven he was there. He straight away knew it was the crazy accountant lady and was coming home to talk properly about it and explain what was going on.

I was so upset by that whole experience, and even once I knew the whole story it was hard for me to get over it. The cover story was very elaborate and seemed way too dangerous and scary for him to be making it up. Ant tried hard to prove his innocence and I guess I believed him in the end. The accountant still rang occasionally, pretending to be someone else. At Christmas, I called her out on it. I was sitting with my family one night when she pretended to be someone. I told her to fuck off… "Oh just, fuck off." She hung up. Then five minutes later she called back on her real number, trying to apologise. She denied all the other times, though. This is a drama that still goes on today, and we can't do anything about it as we can't prove it.

We had a small Christmas party when the studio was finished up for the year and we had a fun night with good friends. The following week, the last week of school was when the bushfires hit. During that week at school, we were on high alert to evacuate and there was a constant smoke cloud around the area. It was really hot and dry, and the air was choking with smoke and we were deep in drought with strict water restrictions. As each day rolled in, so did the smoke and the sky grew darker.

CHAPTER 15

Fire, Flames and Fleeing

It had only been the weekend before that I had made Ant take all the rubbish in my dance trailer to the tip. I thought I may want to use the trailer again soon. Ant hates doing anything around the house and it was a drama to get rid of the rubbish. After a heap of whinging and swearing we took it all to the tip. So glad we did, because three days later the fire hit our road and I had to evacuate. I rushed around, threw things in the trailer, and got the majority of the Christmas presents. I had been packing to go away at Christmas, so, luckily, we had bags for the kids ready to go. I rang Dad to see what it was I had to do... I had received an SMS about the extreme case of fires near us and advising to prepare to leave.

I called Dad to see if he thought that would be the case.

He calmly told me, "Yes, get prepared."

I could see the fire burning over near our neighbour's and the sky was red with black clouds of smoke. As I started to pack the trailer, I received the next message about immediate evacuation. I rang my neighbour and she was a little panicked too. She said the fire was just on the other side of their property, and they were going to stay to protect their farm. They are vegetable farmers so they were staying to save their livelihoods. She told me to get out, though, and said that if the fire came to our property, she would open our gate to let the animals out. We have goats and alpacas.

I ran around frantically, tears streaming down my face. I crazily backed the old car up to the trailer and hooked it up. I got together important paperwork, and grabbed some money that Ant had stashed. Every load to the trailer, I got more hysterical as I looked at the tree line and could see the anger of the fire, looking closer every load. A helicopter was water bombing as I was trying to get the dogs into the trailer and fire trucks were flying down our road. The kids were at preschool and vacation care and they were now calling me as I pulled out of our drive. I spoke to the school. They were being evacuated and could I come and get the kids? I was crying a lot by this point and I told them I was on my way. As I closed the gate behind me, I thought what if this is the last time I see my house? I hoped my animals could get away from the flames.

I had tried to call Ant once, but when he didn't answer, I didn't have time to try again. Dad had called him, though, and had told him what was going on and that he should get home. Ant called me as I pulled up at the preschool. He wanted to know what I was going to do. I said I was getting the kids and heading to Nicole's. She wasn't in the danger zone yet and the roads were pretty blocked to get onto the freeway to leave the area. I grabbed the kids and we headed to Nicole's. Ant was going to try to get home and was planning to hose our place and try to save it.

So many people got evacuated that day and so many lost their homes. Me, the kids and the dogs stayed at Nicole's for the night. Ant stayed at our place, running the hose all night putting out spot fires. We had lost power and the smoke was bad. Roads were closed and the Wollondilly really had turned into a disaster zone. We were very lucky not to have lost our house. Our property was intact, and my animals were safe. Our dogs, Faith and Boo (who was quite sick and old now) were struggling with the heat and smoke. Bulldogs are not good with heat. Overnight at Nicole's, Boo had got worse and I could see she could no longer see and she hadn't eaten anything for a couple of days. Ant came to help me pack up from Nicole's the next day, and help me get Boo into the trailer and help guide me back home as most roads were closed.

We still had no power, and the sky was still dark and smoky. The two water-bomber helicopters were filling up every ten minutes from the dam next door, so it was loud all day. I unpacked and then repacked the van (car). I had planned to leave in a couple of days, but now I was going early the next day for our Christmas break. Late that afternoon, the power came back on. I was planning to do the drive to Lismore at 4am. In the middle of the night, sirens woke us and another notice to evacuate came through to my phone. I sat by my bedroom window for a couple of hours to see the happenings, and at about 2am, I watched the fire trucks leave, so thought I'd get a couple of hours sleep before my nine-hour drive.

I woke from my alarm at 4am and put the last bits into the car, including the kids. Ant wasn't coming. He had to work and I had not wanted him to come, really. With everything that had been going on between us, I thought it would be a nice break and I could just be comfortable with my family. It was just easier without him. Makes it kind of sad to say, but that's how it felt.

The kids were excited by the early dark time start. Andrew sat in the front to keep me company. We arrived in Lismore to the shed (my brother Jimmy lives there now) at about 3.30pm. We had made it. We stayed at the shed for a couple of nights before we moved to Leo's new farm out near Casino. The kids and I were given their granny flat and the kids loved it. We had a wonderful Christmas on the farm. My family had all come and stayed a few days over Christmas. Even our brother, Tom, had come. Tom had been through a break up and his life had been nothing but drama. He had been to jail, he has four kids to a prostitute who he had married, then she had left him to have a baby with a drug addict, taking his four kids and she wouldn't let him see them. I might need a bit more time to go into Tom's back story. So, I will go into his stuff at the end. So yeah, Tom had come to the farm for Christmas and he was now going to stay as a help/farmhand for Leon. All the cousins had a ball running around, swimming in the spa, playing and watching movies, feeding the cows and giant pig and having rides on the quad bikes.

I stayed on for a few days after Christmas, then headed to the Gold Coast where I had booked me, the kids and Mum and Dad into a kids' resort for five nights. On the way up, I went and collected Ant from the airport. He was joining us. The rest of the holiday went okay, but Ant was moody and lazy and disrespected me a lot in front of my parents. It was awkward, and I didn't know what to do anymore for it not to be this way. He had missed us while we were away but as soon as we were back together, he would get angry and rude. He had no patience for the kids and when asked to do something to help, he loses it.

We had New Year's up there and Jane, her kids and her new man (Jane was going through a divorce – she had cheated on Damon and fallen in love with this man) came as well. We headed back to Sydney after the five days. Our neighbours had been feeding and watering our animals. It had been extremely hot and we were still in drought. I dropped Ant at his friend's place to pick up his car on the way through, so I was arriving home by myself. When I arrived, I was shocked by the dead grass, dead garden and everything looked so thirsty. At the gate was Faith, jumping around like the young boofy bulldog she is, and Boo was at her feet curled up in a ball. Faith was kicking up dust and stepping on Boo, and she wasn't moving.

I flew out of the car. "Boo, Boo!" She didn't respond. She looked dead and I started crying. I reached her and touched her and she put her head up. I spoke softly to her, "Boo, come on girl." She was laying in the sun and I wanted to move her to the shade. Her eyes were completely covered in white now, and she couldn't hear either. I lead her to her dog house, sat and patted her a while, and brought her water. I sat crying for my Boo. It was the end for her. I knew it and I couldn't let her suffer anymore. She had been the best dog. She had survived cancer, had survived puppies and a uterus infection. She had the most beautiful personality and once Penny had died, we had decided to get another Australian Bulldog. That's how we came to get Faith.

When Ant got home that night, I explained how I had found Boo and that she needed to go to the vets and be put down tomorrow. I had also discovered that three of my chickens were dead. The heat had made them just drop dead. It was a rather devasting sight to come home to. Fires were still burning around the area, and the air was hot and dry. We just needed rain.

Boo was put to rest the next day. I couldn't go. There was no way I was going to be able to handle it. Ant drove her away in his car and two hours later came back. He stayed with her while she had her needle and patted her until the end. Faith had a hard time adjusting to life without Boo. Faith loves dog company and didn't want much to do with humans and now she didn't have a companion.

We buried Boo's ashes under the gumtree in the paddock next to Penny. I can see the tree from our kitchen window.

CHAPTER 16

Here We Are

It probably was a good indication (the start) that 2020 was not going to be great. I had high expectations. I didn't think a year could be as bad as 2019. Here we were though, things starting negative and sad.

I had my registration day at the studio in January and we were able to get more students. We doubled our numbers so it was looking promising. I went back to work, back to the gym. I was by my lonesome at my gym now, as all the girls had jumped on the F45 bandwagon and were obsessed there. It did eventually rain and it flooded, of course, and businesses had to close for the clean-up. The grass turned green though, and all the bushfire damage turned from black to bright green.

Leo started transition at the College and his medication helped him settle most days. Tristan went into year one a little apprehensive at first, because of the new class, new teacher thing. Andrew started year five and was happy with his teacher for the year. Marly started three days a week in daycare and she also started ballet with me. Tristan also dances, doing hip hop and boys' tap. Andrew keeps up his hip hop and started boys' tap. Leo tried to do dancing but he couldn't concentrate and caused trouble, so he got asked by me to not come back for a while. Term 1 of 2020 started out busy as usual and we were going along, planning the year and our end-of-year cruise. Then BOOM.

Covid-19, yep, Coronavirus took over our lives. Well, stopped our lives, really. I had to close the studio, the gyms closed, our favourite cafes and the pubs closed. Everything closed and then we were cut off from our people. Lockdown, social isolation. The weekend before full isolation, Nicole and her family came over. We drank and carried on. Then we could no longer visit each other and we were stuck in our houses with our kids, home-schooling. I felt I had lost everything, everything I had worked for and built. I felt lost, and didn't know what to do. Ant negotiated my rent for the studio to get three months free so that was a little less worry.

Then my good friend and adult student, Claire, decided to help me keep my business alive. Probably not grow, but okay, until we come out the other side of the Corona. Claire was a godsend and so motivating for me... she sorted out my website to set up the online learning. Her husband set up the studio for filming and every week since the outbreak, we have been filming and uploading dance classes, six new ones a week. I haven't made money from the classes but it's kept my students dancing through this time. I have gained new online dancers too. I'm at school working, supervising high school kids that have had to return to school already.

That pretty much brings us to current day, May 2020. We are desperate for some normalness back in our lives. I want to go to the pub. I want to socialise and eat at a restaurant. I want to be able to escape sometimes and have somewhere to go.

I'm not sure what the outcome of mine and Ant's story is. It's our 15-year wedding anniversary tomorrow. He admitted to me recently that he hadn't been taking his medication but he is taking them again now. It's a constant rollercoaster, with a heap of downs. I hate being in a relationship with a person who is like this. You never know what mood or what Ant you're going to get. I know I love him because I wouldn't have put up with this for so long. I'm so worried though, that by putting up with the way things are, that I'm enabling the behaviour, that I'm hurting my kids by his actions and attitude, but then it's not me. I'm just staying with him. I also get sad thinking about what I could have, or what I would like. By staying, am I missing out on meeting a person who will love me and treat me wonderfully? I just don't know.

Living with hope that this will all pass soon and I will be back in the studio, doing what I love. Living with hope that my kids are going to be okay and will grow into adjusted, even well-adjusted, adults. That Ant will snap out of it and we might be happy again. Life throws too many shit curveballs my way that I feel I'm always looking over my shoulder. When things are okay for a period of time, I'm nervous for the fallout, for when it doesn't last. It's like I'm always waiting for the bad times. I don't want to live that way anymore and I would love to feel comfortable in my life, in my relationship and feel as though I have a little bit of control over what happens in my life.

I'm pretty sure I have missed things out in my story and it's a little hard to remember everything and dates. But think I captured most of the important events and how my life has played out so far. As I finish writing this part of my book I do so in my supervision time at school during this whole Covid-19 pandemic. We are slowly coming out of lockdown and this week the schools are returning. By Friday this week, cafes will re-open but only ten people are allowed at a time.

I'm not a hundred per cent sure of how to conclude my story or if it is completed yet. It has been therapeutic for me to write it all out. I didn't want it to be a massive sob story but I'm definitely aware of the way in which events have shaped my life and the way I feel about certain things and how I have come to develop those emotions. I am grateful for the wonderful people in my life, people who support, inspire, care, are positive and selfless. People who check in on me. As I get older and wiser, I know my constant stresses in life are not easy for people to be around all the time, so I like to try and sit back a little more and let everyone tell their stories and enjoy their moments. I have a constant grey cloud that follows me around these days and I'm not sure a higher dosage of my happy pills would work. I like to describe my grey cloud as the misty, foggy past that keeps following me, always with a chance of rain. Occasionally, you get glimpses of the sunshine but only when the wonderful people around me step me out into the shine.

Changing my life to a life of more sunshine is, I know, up to me. Only I can do it. I don't want to just cope every day. Coping does not equal happy. I just haven't worked out the how of happy yet or if it even exists! I'm hoping the next chapter of my life is one of fulfilment, contentment, peace and love. I still believe in the fairytale love, the Mills and Boon love, even. I know everyone changes throughout their lifetime and experiences and the people you have those experiences with is how we evolve into the new person we are today.

I miss me, though. I miss the young, happy, slightly hyperactive, funny, a little bit loud girl I was before. Before life knocked me about a bit. The excitement of life or the expectation of what life was perhaps going to look like for me. Being confident in myself to speak up. The Nikki of anticipation and lack of patience, saying what sprung to mind, sometimes just saying things to see people be uncomfortable. I remember an innocence and an ignorance thinking that all I had to do was be me and work hard and I would be happy. I don't have regrets, really, because I wouldn't be the person I am today without my mistakes. I really wish I had kissed Jed back in high school, that's probably a regret I have.

Today, I want happiness for me and my family. It's kind of sounding like a wish list now. Anyway, the next chapter of my life needs to be filled with laughter, passion, creativity, peace, security and an overall sense of calm. I have way too many busy minds that fill my house. A calmness to our storm of a household would definitely lead to some kind of happiness for me, I think. Coping, I hope will be really out of fashion, like so 2018. I'm going to excel at life. I have got to. It's my road to happiness.

Oh, how I wish these past few pages really were the conclusion of my story so far but alas they are not — and I can say now looking back to 2020 that shit was about to come in a massive downpour and send my world into piles of ruins.

CHAPTER 17

The Trouble with Tom

I was going to go back into the details of my brother, Tom.

After Tom moved to Dad's cousin Pearl's full-time, he had a great childhood, was spoilt and loved. His non biological father, Richard, was diagnosed with Parkinson's and his health deteriorated quickly. He passed away early into Tom's teens. He had a great relationship with Richard, so this knocked him around a bit emotionally. Pearl, also struggled with the loss of her husband. Tom started acting out, causing more problems locally and at home, not listening, roaming the streets. He got into trouble a lot for vandalising and assault. The small town of Evans Head knew of him and the police often brought him home. Tom would come and stay with Dad on the farm at times but he would often disappear.

Pearl ended up getting a new boyfriend and started going away a lot. She ended kicking Tom out, probably having finally lost patience with his shit. Dad went and got him and took him to the farm. He wouldn't stay, though. He roamed the streets of Lismore. He stole money from Dad and had people bashing him up on a regular basis.

He moved into town at some point after one of his court cases was over. He got a disability pension and moved into the bad side of town in a caravan park in an old caravan. He lived pay cheque to pay cheque, was robbed regularly, bashed a lot and became addicted to ice. My other brothers, Dylan and Leon, tried a few times to go and get him out of that caravan park and away from the drugs. They even went with Dad once and kicked all the other leeches out of the place. Tom occasionally came home after he had got beaten really bad or needed money. However, this ordeal went on for years. He ended up meeting his wife, at some stage through this time. She was working in Lismore for a bit but visiting from Wollongong. It later came out she had been working in a brothel and that's how she met Tom. She had come on a working holiday to her other prostitute friend's place in Lismore. She came with her two boys who had different dads. Anyway, she ended up taking Tom back to Wollongong with her as she claimed she was now pregnant with his child. They moved into a housing commission place and often rang family for money. Nan was the one who often gave them money over the years because she felt sorry for the kids. They went on to get married a few years into the relationship and four kids in. Everyone in the family had pretty much had had enough of the Tom and his crazy wife saga. They kept getting pregnant and crying poor and telling lies all the time. I lived the closest, so I went to the wedding and Dad did. Dylan, I think did, and Summa flew down for it.

After a few more years of drama and fights with them, we decided to not talk to them anymore. Until 2018 when they split up, she left him on the side of the road at the Gold Coast. Tom told us that they had taken the kids for a holiday, when she had attacked him one night and took all his money. We learnt from Tom that she had kicked him out a week before the holiday because she was having sex with someone else and wanted him out, but then asked him to come back because she couldn't look after the kids herself. He loved his kids and went back to her. They had six kids at this stage. When she left him on the side of the road in Queensland, she took all his things with her. He had his phone but no charger, but he managed to call Dad. He slept on the street overnight, and Dad transferred him some money and he got back to Lismore for a couple of days. He then ended up in North Queensland. He had got a ride up there with someone and he was back on the drugs.

That was the last we heard or saw of Tom until end of 2019. Summa somehow had got in contact with him and I believe he had spoken to Nan. He had just got out of jail. He had gone to jail for driving offences, and his wife had gone to Queensland to get him. He had gone back to her and she had him basically looking after all the kids while she went out every day with her boyfriend. She even had him picking the kids up from school in the van. Tom didn't have a licence, so got caught a few times driving and that's how he ended up in jail. His wife had moved her new boyfriend into their place and she was now pregnant to him.

When Tom got out of jail, he wanted to see his kids badly and she wouldn't allow it. He got a flat in a housing block not too far away. She allowed him to see the kids when it suited her. His flat was disgusting. He had no furniture and often couldn't feed his kids if they did visit. He had some neighbours who had kids and who helped him out with some toys, food when it was end of pay week and someone also lent him a TV. He was also given some mattresses. She would drop the kids to him without notice and not pick them up for days. He was happy to have his kids and they preferred him to being at home. It was just before Christmas 2019 that Summa spoke to all the siblings about Tom's situation and how it would be good to get him up to the family (Lismore) for Christmas. She also wanted us to make a fund for Tom to get some things for his place and his kids.

Tom organised a train ticket. However, his crazy wife showed up with the kids two days before he was due to leave and it seems that she knew he was going. She didn't come back for the kids for a week, so Tom missed his train. Dad had gone to the station at the other end at 3am but he didn't come. Summa jumped back onto him and blasted him about it. DO NOT TELL HER. He booked another ticket and left that night, with Summa ringing him multiple times on the trip up to check he was still on the train.

Tom arrived, and came out to the shed where I was staying with the kids at Christmas. I was shocked when I saw him. He had teeth missing, a broken nose and scars. It had only been two weeks earlier that someone had come and attacked him at his flat. He said he believed it was someone associated with his ex-wife. Someone had hit him in the back of the head with a pole and smashed his face too.

Over Christmas, Tom was great. He really is good with kids, probably because he is like one mentally. He then stayed on at Leo's and worked on the farm. His ex ended up sending up two of his boys, saying he could have them. They moved into the granny flat with Tom and started at the local school. That's where Tom met a new love and he soon moved off the farm into her place. He seems to be doing okay. He will always be drama, I think, but at least he is doing better now and he has two of his kids. He is still living in Casino with his new girlfriend and he seems happy. So that's Tom's story... well a quick rundown.

CHAPTER 18

The Delay of my New Chapter

The hope and optimism that things were to get better for me and my life's journey back in 2020–21 were smashed and sent packing and my fight to survive really had to kick in. Just when I thought my story could just bob along the bumpy road I had been dealt and I had completed all I had to write out of my head, more shit arrived.

My trust in people and life failed me again — and I have been struggling to swim out of this last bad dumping.

The last week of term 2, 2020 I was busy trying to get dancing back off the ground. Trying to expand the studio, welcoming new students and trying to navigate my business again. I was busy working a lot and trying to make sure the kids didn't miss their dad too much as he had started to frequently not come home. When he was home, he was not really there, sleeping all day or sitting drugged out on the lounge. I'm pretty sure he has a drug problem; uppers at night and then painkillers to make him dreg out (think I may have made up that word). Anyway, he disappeared for real. Ant got up one morning and told me he had to go to Canberra, saying he would be back the next day. He was gone for three days and his cousin was looking for him, worried. I didn't know what to do, wondering how long I was supposed to wait before I reported him missing. I felt I sat rather calmly waiting for news through his cousin. Ant did show up eventually and was rather mean and angry at me for trying to find him.

It was exactly two days after the emotional turmoil of that and I was at school /work for the day. I had headed straight to the studio after school for my afternoon classes. Marly was due to come do her Ballet class, however she never turned up. Reanne, the nanny, hadn't turned up with her. After her class had finished and as soon as I could get a chance to call, I rang Reanne's phone. She didn't answer — the police did.

"Do you know Reanne?" the constable on the other end asked.

"Um, yes," I said.

"She has been in an accident," he replied.

"What?" I replied, shocked. "Where are my kids?"

"She was picking up your kids?" he asked. "There are no kids in the car. Reanne is okay, but she has gone in the ambulance to the hospital."

I was in shock, confused as to why she was in the main street of Picton at pick up time, it was too far for her to be down there. Unless she had the accident on her way to my place. Where are the kids? It was late now ...they were supposed to be picked up by 4pm. I left Nicole to continue my classes as I jumped in my car and headed to pick them up. I was met at the door of the centre with shocked faces. The staff had seen videos of the car accident on social media and knew it had been my car (van) that was involved. I sat with the staff as they showed me the videos that witnesses had uploaded of my car swerving all over the road, crashing into cars, walls all the way into the middle of Picton, where eventually Reanne had a head-on with a four-wheel drive, right outside the front of the local school.

Social media was going crazy. People had recognised my car and I had to constantly tell people it wasn't me driving. So many months of no answers and no toxicity report. I had gone to clean out the van at the smash repairs and had found empty bottles of cider, witnesses had said they could smell the alcohol on her when they pulled her out of the car. She constantly denied it and argued that they didn't take her licence from her, so she couldn't have been drunk but the toxicity report did come back saying high range alcohol present. I couldn't talk to her. But I noticed Ant took a great interest in what had happened and even helped Reanne with finding legal help I was so confused, so hurt.

She tried multiple times to contact me in private to explain but I was so mad and my trust had been shattered. I later discovered that she had a reaction to drugs Ant had supplied her with, that she had taken the night before. She lost her licence for 6 months.

Ant at some point went into a drug rehabilitation centre for a few weeks. While he was in there, I found a new business for him to give him some purpose and to keep him local. I had hopes of having him around a lot more and getting him away from the shit he was caught up in due to his failed business dealings with bad people. The business was an uber driving type business for our local area. He seemed better when he got out of Rehab and threw himself into the business. He was struggling to meet the demand for a driver by himself and needed more drivers. He recruited his long-lost cousin who came to help him out at peak times. Ant was also helping to re build my new studio.

Sadly, Ant's behaviour started to deteriorate, and again he wouldn't come home and his moods were hostile when he was home. Emotional abuse was normal and financial abuse seemed the best form for him, he thrived on the control. He threw things in rage, punched holes in walls and cut me deep with his words. His favourite words for me were DOG CUNT. I separated from him, but we still lived under the same roof at this point. The separation came about after our family trip to Copeton Dam in January 2021.

We hired a caravan over the New year in 2021 and headed out to Copeton Dam for water skiing and camping with my family. The night before we left, Ant had finished driving the uber and had come home with his cousin (he was going to be staying while we were away). Ant was overly agitated, paranoid and flipping out a lot. I wasn't sure what was going on with him, so his cousin ended up giving him a Xanax and this calmed him down and he soon passed out. The following day he slept while I packed the caravan and the car. By mid-afternoon, Ant had come around and was feeling good he said.

We picked the kids up from vacation care and started on our drive north, it was pouring down with rain. The kids were excited to be going on holidays and were mucking around a lot in the back. Ant was driving and he started a twitch which seemed to get worse as the kids agitated him more. Then came outbursts of strange noises almost like how I imagine someone who has Tourette Syndrome. He got worse as we progressed north and then he started swerving all over the road and his noises increased. The kids were now upset and were begging him to pull over and let me drive, but he seemed to not hear what was being said to him.

Sometime just after 9pm I was able to convince him to pull over into a truck stop. We set the caravan up for sleeping and the kids went off to sleep. Ant had calmed down since we stopped, but then he started complaining about his head and a striking pain. I took him out to the picnic tables outside near the public toilets. From there I witnessed Ant as a seriously lost man mentally. I cried a lot as I watched him stagger around the truck stop, fighting imaginary people, swearing and talking to himself. I would beg him to stop or shake him at times, and at times he would come back telling me that he loved me and it would be okay, then his eyes would roll back and he would slip back into his swearing and muttering.

This went on for an hour, and then he started contorting and trying to get back into the van. I stressed about the kids seeing him this way and him waking them. I went to my shower bag and pulled out the extra Xanax tablets Ant's cousin had given me the night before — for emergency only, he had told me. I gave Ant the Xanax and a Valium that his doctor had prescribed him. I then pushed him into the back seat of the car and closed the door. I stood in the rain and watched him contort and fit in the back seat for a couple of minutes. Returning to the van, I sat on the edge of our bed feeling the jerks and bumps of his fits in the attached car. Shock and devastation filled me. I was so scared.

It was about midnight by this time and I messaged Mum to tell her our whereabouts, or where I thought we were, and what had happened. I just wanted someone to know where to look for us if we didn't make it the next day. The jolts subsided and I went out to see if he was okay. He had passed out in a contorted and very uncomfortable-looking way but I could see he was breathing. So that he wouldn't suffocate I opened the back door of the car slightly and went back to the van.

At some point in the early hours, he came into the van and fell asleep next to me in the bed. I didn't sleep at all; I listened to him snore and the van shook from trucks screaming past on the freeway. When the morning rolled around Ant was quiet and calm. He didn't remember anything from the night before and he wasn't overly keen to talk about it or explain. He promised to phone his doctor to have a consult about it. We safely arrived at the Dam and I was relieved to be with my family. For the week we were there, Ant was distant and slept most of the time. The kids had a great time though, swimming, boating, running around with their cousins and not showering.

When we packed up and left the Dam things were a little tense between Ant and I, we travelled half way back to Sydney and stopped for the night just outside of Tamworth and then did the rest of the trip the next day home. As soon as we rolled into our driveway at Bargo, Ant perked up and jumped out of the car. He was gone within an hour of us returning. He rang later that night saying the van was due back to hire people the next day and so it needed to be unpacked and cleaned. Luckily, I had spent the afternoon unpacking it. He didn't come home that night but he picked up the van the next morning and took it back to the hirers. This was the last time I saw him before he disappeared.

For the next two weeks my life was a mess of lies, speculation and confusion. After a week of Ant not contacting me and me finding out some weird stories from some strange people, I was very confused as to what was real and what wasn't. Stories of double lives, drugs, prostitution and general deceit left me in a state of mental mush. Ant's cousin had stayed on to keep running the business. Little did I know then (I do now) that the cousin was also a very sick person mentally and he was sabotaging the business and trying to frame Ant or extort him for money. Ant often spoke in riddles and I had a hard time understanding what he was trying to get at. I feel now he was trying to tell me things without being unfaithful to his cousin.

The entire time he was there, the cousin wanted to stay in the house with me and the kids. He kept dropping hints about not making any money and he needed money, he possibly wanted to take over Ant's life. The kids were creeped out by him and I couldn't stand having to have him around let alone stay in our house.

Anyway, what a mess ... I put a missing person's report out on Ant. I threw out all his things, tried to sell all his Swiss watches and made a statement to start an AVO order.

Eventually, Ant came out of hiding with many delusions of why he had disappeared. He was paranoid and drug addiction looked to have played a part. He told me stories of private jets and dodgy dealings in Byron Bay, saying he couldn't contact us and that he was trying to keep us safe. I wouldn't allow him to come home — I spoke to his parents and said he had to go to rehab and would have to live with them. I explained to them he wasn't safe to be around the kids and I didn't want his rage in the house. He tried to come to visit to explain himself and just turned up at the house. My dad was staying with me at the time, the kids were at vacation care and I was at a promotion day for SSDA. The babysitter, Marly and Nicole's daughter were at the house when Ant turned up. He sent everyone into a panic because he wasn't making any sense and tried to stop my dad from leaving. Dad was moving stuff from house to new studio. Ant had stopped him in the driveway, trying to explain things to my dad and show him evidence of his paranoia as to why he was away. He had police tapes and a photo of the Byron Bay sign.

All this mess has left me scarred. I no longer know truth. I'm confused a lot, sad and longing for happiness even more. After this storm settled a little, Ant began living with his parents, leaving me trying to find my feet again. We thought Ant finally got a proper diagnosis — psychosis?

CHAPTER 19

The Truth?

Over the next six months, I took Ant back in and we tried to patch things up. He continued watching over the build of the dance studio and working in the uber driving business. He bought in his young worker from the Pizza shop to help him drive, Hayley. She would work the weekends when it was busy and he needed an extra car. She also worked really hard to become my friend, helping me with the kids and getting in my ear about all the things Ant was up to. This proved, of course, to be the way to make sure I didn't find out about Ant and her having an affair for 4.5 years. I ended up tracking down the old accountant friend from pizza shop days and she had all the evidence I needed, along with the stories and unexplained chance encounters. When the Accountant became aware of this sick affair, she had become obsessed about it and catching them out. She had screenshots of messages between them and Instagram posts of dates they went on when I was away with the kids. Ant was often cut out of the photo but you could see his watch, arm or a shoe.

They had been fucking since Hayley was sixteen. It makes me sick that it may have happened even before she was sixteen as she was only fifteen when she started working for him.

This whole thing came to light the same week Ant got caught and charged for drug trafficking. He got done around the corner from the studio in the middle of the day. Hayley came to the studio later that night to tell me he was in jail. When the detectives came to question me about it a few days later, they informed me about Hayley and Ant using the driving business as a transportation / delivery system for the drugs. The head detective knew of Hayley well and was aware of how they had started an affair when she was young and working for Ant. Small world we live in, the head detective had known Hayley when she was in high school and she had been close to his daughter. The detectives also informed me about how my dance studio had been used as a drug safe house for dealers and told me about the quantities of certain drugs that had been hidden and where. Someone had been talking in jail about it, someone who had been involved and was now trying to get a reduced sentence.

I had to really beg to prove my stupidness in the whole situation and about how I didn't know and how sick I felt by everything they had just told me. They did actually believe me and knew I must not have known. They just thought I might be a woman scorned and be able and willing to give them a bit more information.

Ant was on very strict bail conditions and he was still living at home, although he hated having to be home a lot and being required to check in at the police station. He soon hated being trapped at home since we were in the second Covid lockdown with strict curfew rules as well. He wanted away from me and the kids — so, in a rage and hissing at me through clenched teeth he moved to Bankstown with one of his dodgy mates, to an apartment, breaking all the Covid lockdown laws. That dodgy mate later stole a lot of our property and kicked Ant out. Ant was asked to leave because of the way he constantly partied, lived in filth and moved Hayley in. All the while, Ant denied the affair with Hayley, gaslighting me, trying to make out I was crazy and bitter. Hayley jumped on the bandwagon trying to convince me I was insane and that they just work together and that I'm a stupid old woman, bored and lonely blah blah.

So many lies and pain at this time. I couldn't trust anyone, so many things came out that I had a hard time focusing on anything. Every time I would discover or uncover a lie, a new issue or betrayal was waiting to step in and knock me around again. My whole life unravelled before me — I could see how certain situations and what had been told to me to be the truth was not. I could see my past negative experiences with Ant and what was going on at the time and the lies that were told to cover up. Encounters with people in his life or friendships made were all a façade.

I had so much embarrassment, pain and anger. I was crushed, the kids watched me crumble, Andrew especially experienced the worst of it and helped me through my trauma. When I couldn't stop crying and I couldn't get off the floor, Andrew would call Mum and Dad and put them on the phone to me to pep-talk me. They would tell Andrew to, "Get Mum a wine and just sit with her."

I didn't dwell on my betrayal and misery for long — I couldn't — I had four kids to care for and I wanted to make sure they didn't feel the impact of the fallout. I worked extra hard to make things as normal as possible for them. They didn't even notice for a few weeks that their dad didn't live with us anymore. When I did tell them there wasn't much emotion for them, they knew I was the one that did everything for them anyway and that life would be the same really.

Ant's anger and verbal, financial abuse intensified. He wouldn't discuss selling the farm and wouldn't help me out financially as he saw the fact the kids and I weren't paying the mortgage on the property and were living there as a good reason that he didn't need to give me any money. Every time I spoke to him on the phone he blew up and wouldn't listen to what I wanted, which was to leave the property. I couldn't maintain it, couldn't pay the owing rates, couldn't get fences fixed, paddocks slashed etc., I slowly sold off things that were of no use or didn't work to try and get some money together, I couldn't pay school fees or the fines from council from my animals constantly escaping.

CHAPTER 20

The Gap Year

Ant's constant need to control me became very evident in the following months. He rang me constantly, first being all nice in conversation and then when he didn't hear what he wanted to hear from me he would fly into a rage. I had approached his family about money and if they could convince Ant to help me out financially. Ant's Dad told me not to ask Ant for money as he didn't have any, and that he was using everything he had for lawyer fees for his criminal case. I pleaded with his parents about convincing him to sell the property. His father was on the title of the property as he was fifty per cent owner with Ant and he didn't want to sell it either because it was going to one day make them multi-millionaires. Ant's dad talked me into not taking legal action to sell the property by saying that he would give me money to survive. Even promising to buy me and the kids a house later. However, that never happened as he couldn't get a loan to buy me a house and I got cut off from Ant's family because I had him charged.

One afternoon, Ant rang when I was picking kids up from school, speaking to the kids on loud speaker. He was trying to be all happy nice guy and asking the kids if they wanted him to come home to live yet, trying to persuade them to say yes. I hung up on him and called him back once I was out of the car and away from the kids. I told him no way because I was done with him and I had just started dating someone. This was true, fresh by three weeks at that time.

This launched him into a massive meltdown, screaming all types of things to me: Slut! Dog cunt! I kept hanging up on him and he called back over thirty times and messaged abuse also. He demanded to know who I was dating. I didn't tell him... but he still threatened to kill me and put me in a hole along with the person I was fucking. Andrew had heard the threat and said, "Mum, you have got to call the police."

I took out an AVO and Ant was arrested the next day. This sent his family into a spin and talking badly about me, how I had over-reacted and as if Ant would ever hurt me.

As the new year rolled around, in 2022 I was still dating Danny. He was constantly scared and nervous for his life but he hung around and was helping me find a rental property so I could get out of the financial control that Ant had on me. Danny ended up moving in with me and the kids when we found a house in the area a few kilometres up the road. He had just lost his place and was going to help me out with sharing the rent. At the end of February, during the floods we packed and fled the property to five kilometres away to the rental place.

I didn't tell Ant we had moved, however, he knew as he had me followed regularly. All was going well in the new place. I felt I had regained some control. The kids moved to the local public school so I didn't have to pay fees. The kids liked our new place I was able to take most of my animals as we had four acres. It felt like a small win and a little freedom. However, this didn't last long as Ant moved exactly one kilometre away — to the end of my road.

Danny and I just slipped into a domestic relationship, he helped me a lot with the kids and kept the house going while I worked constantly. My business was struggling to recover properly after the second Covid lockdown and then when I reopened in September 2021 it was only two months before the first flood, with another flood in February 2022. The studio sits on the main street of Picton and close to the river. Water came under the doors, but we were able to keep in off the dance floor. My landlord was an old grumpy and stingy man, and although the roof leaked a lot, he wouldn't repair it properly. The electricals went in the backrooms. In May of 2022 I had to let go of most of my staff keeping only another teacher to help run classes. We closed the café and the creche because I couldn't afford to pay my staff any more. The landlord increased my rent, doubled it actually, and I was drowning in debt. I was back working at the high school to keep afloat and be able to feed my kids.

Danny and I were struggling as I did not have time for him, he was extremely needy, he didn't work and soon the cracks of his past started to show up. He had a drug problem, which is what probably gave him the money problems. He stopped paying his share of rent and didn't tell me. When I did find out we were behind a few thousand dollars and it was up to me to try and catch it up. Things with Danny got extremely bad, so we broke up but remained living together. Sometime in July is when we ended — around the same time my girlfriends took me out for drinks and gave me an intervention. Knowing all my struggles they sat me down pre drinks and said I needed to move to Cairns at the top of Queensland, to the tropics. Break the toxic cycle I was trapped in. Dad had said the same thing to me two weeks prior, telling me it was ''time to come home, enough was enough'' except not to Lismore as they would be moving to Cairns as soon as they sold the Farm. I brushed it off at the time. Now the girls were telling me the same thing. I cried a lot thinking everyone was so sick of all my drama and they wanted me gone.

However, I actually thought yes, they were right — the only way out of the dark place I had found myself in was to head to the sunshine and put distance between. The wheels were in motion.

I moved the dance concert forward to end of September with the intention of leaving to head north just before Christmas. Time enough for a manager to take on my clients at dancing, so as to not leave my SSDA family in the lurch. I put my notice in with both landlords at the studio and the house. After the concert I sold off a lot of stuff in the studio, took what I could and closed the doors during the first week of October.

By November my shipping container had arrived and Danny helped me pack, helped me sell off some stuff. Ant was up to his usual shit and the week before I was due to leave, he breached his AVO conditions and then same day sent men in balaclavas to bash Danny, thinking that I had left in my car when in fact it was Danny who had left the house in my car. Within 20 minutes of Danny leaving an unmarked Mitsubishi Lancer drove up my driveway. A man got out of the car heading to my garage, which was always open and where Danny always hung out it was sort of his mancave space. The man was calling out, "Hey bro, hey bro."

I went to the front door and called out to the man waiting in the Lancer, "Can I help you?"

The driver started beeping, then the covered man came running out of the garage and dove into the back seat and they raced off down the driveway, almost getting bogged on the way out. I was left shaking, confused but knowing it must have been Ant. It had been that morning when I had a fight with him when he was picking up the kids and he went on about Danny and money and sped off dangerously with the kids. I was screaming after him in the driveway and even the neighbours came running out. Danny had called the police. The police came out to get a statement from me but I didn't want to give one as I thought it would just make things worse and I was so close to leaving for the sunshine anyway. The police left a little pissed at me but said if I changed my mind to call and they would come back.

So, after the visit from the thug-heads I did change my mind. I couldn't prove the thug visit was for its intended purpose but I was able to make my statement. When the kids got back from their visit with their dad he was arrested again, he spent 48 hours in jail and was then released again. Ant admitted to Andrew he sent the thugs around but it was to just talk to Danny and give him a phone hmm sure, in balaclavas!

Ant had done so many dodgy things that I couldn't prove over the previous 12 months. He had Hayley break in and steal things, she followed me often, he always knew what was going on and began calling Andrew at times asking who was such and such at the front gate, why was I selling the car and so on. He would accuse me of selling things of his and then when I would tell him no I didn't I will show you and you can pick it up whenever, the items would already be gone. He would already have taken them, meaning he had broken into the house and stolen them. The mind games were relentless. It was time to go!

CHAPTER 21

Here I Begin

The build up to and stress of the move came to head the day I left Wollondilly. A sadness swept over me as I looked at my badly packed trailer. Danny had helped me to the end but was angry and aggressive the morning I was leaving. He started to throw the remaining things to be packed into the trailer, breaking stuff and spitting ugly words at me. I drove off, heading to Ant's to pick up the kids from their last visit with him. I cried on the way to his house, thinking of all I was leaving behind, all my achievements that had died off, my friends, my animals that all had to be rehomed. I dried my face before I got out of the car and collected the kids and they seemed excited as we drove down and out of Picton for our last time.

We spent a week travelling up the east coast, staying in motels and cabins. Our belongings had left a few days before us in the shipping container and I was able to secure a new rental in Cairns. We arrived in Cairns — me, the four kids and a sad-looking trailer that had been battered all the way up the coast by torrential rain, so much so that some of our things were floating. We had arrived with a fresh feeling of hope and calmness. I headed to Summa's in the north of Cairns to recoup for a couple of days before Craig and his mates were going to help us move into our house and unpack the container. I felt a calmness fill me; I was a little unsettled with the how I was going to do this but Summa and Craig gave me a sense of hope and strength in that I had come this far the rest would be easy now.

We moved into our place in Redlynch on the 3rd of December 2022. We were so excited to see our new area. A beautiful newly built house amongst a brand-new suburban estate. Surrounded by fresh water creeks and rainforest, between the towering lush forest-covered mountains of the tropics. It really feels like paradise to me. The kids walk to school every day as it is only 150 metres from our front door.

We spent the remainder of the holidays exploring our new habitat and spent a fair bit of time in our new home setting up and settling in. I was extremely poor, all my money had gone towards the move and paying off the debts before I left. Ant gave me no help until I cried a lot and begged. He did the four weeks of a payment that had been agreed on, then he cut me off again. I borrowed from everyone, well family mainly, and by the end of those Christmas holidays I owed about $6,000 to family members and that was purely to get me to my new job start date.

I had secured a contract teaching dance at Cairns State High and started working there at the end of January, and then working casual on my days off as a relief teacher as I was badly in need of money. Although I am poor and I have to constantly worry about money and how to make it through a fortnight before next pay, I can say I am happier here. I'm free. My hip gives me grief and I pray to get a new one very soon, still sitting on that waiting list. I love my job and have a new passion or new restored passion for dance education. I'm slowly looking ahead to start Shooting Stars again with one location and day locked in so far for term three. The kids are very happy and seem to enjoy the new life. It's only when their dad visits and buys them everything at a click of the fingers that puts a little strain on me as they know they can't have everything with me. However, I do feel they understand more now about what is involved for mum to be able to get them new shoes, or take them out for dinner. If something goes wrong with the car or the internet bill is due, they understand now that means a quiet weekend will be on the cards.

For the first time in a really long time, I have hope for our future, and I have a strength that sometimes surprises me. I'm proud of me. I now know after this journey of my life so far that I have done a lot, overcome a lot and kept on rolling with each and every storm that came my way. I like to think I danced through it, actually sometimes it was a solum dance of sadness with my stage dark and my soul alone. Other times I attacked my challenges pirouetting and jete-ing onto the next challenge.

I am so grateful for some of the people that joined my dance along the way for however long it was that they joined me. It meant my journey, my dance, was not a solo for the whole show. Now I'm here my dance has not finished and my journey goes on, my focus on peace and love of my kids. I do feel lonely and hope to meet my next dance partner soon. Someone who is really good at lifting me up and giving me truth, a beautiful soul that wants to sway with me and hold me close. There's that Mills and Boon romance again.

This is the letter I wrote to Ant to release him from me.

The Letter

Antonio,

I have finally had time and space, it has been time and distance that has healed me. I can finally breathe and can now release, each day I find myself becoming me again. I'm no longer depressed, I can find light in most of my days and I'm lighter in my soul.

I need to release you from my soul. We may have entered this life to be connected in a soul contract but now that journey has ended and whatever lessons in this life you needed me for my job is done. I get to find happiness now and be calm to see out my days here. I truly believe I served you a purpose and although it was extremely painful for me, I have learned a lot from our time together — I guess your purpose for me.

You gave me my children and that I am forever grateful. You forced me to be strong, resilient, capable. Conditioning me to be tough and know how to do it all alone.

I know all the things you hid from me and stole. You were never the right man for me. You have always hidden yourself. Your real self. I don't think I ever saw the real Ant. Not until the end, when you were finally exposed. You have taught me how to see through bullshit and how to never trust. I know that Karma really does exist and it all catches up in the end. Strange encounters with people that I had even forgot existed or how I even knew them have popped up to just to explain things to me, signs that I missed along the way. How my gut feeling about certain situations were correct and I should have listened to my gut. I will now always listen to my Gut. If I had done that, I would have saved myself many years of emotional torture from you.

You taught me to how to love unconditionally even though I didn't feel it in return. I think you thought you did, but it was difficult for you with your Narcissism. It's hard for you to see and feel beyond your own needs and wants. I learned how to adapt to your behaviour, changed myself to try and please you and your mood, your wants, everything on your terms. I didn't even realise I was doing it at the time, slowly each year forgetting myself and what I needed and wanted.

You picked me knowing I could fit the mould of being a good enough person, and not morally corrupt, to suit the persona you were wanting to portray to the world. My energy is vibrant, and I was happy, clean and wholesome. You found me at my most confident and happy. You subtly and slowly - through betrayal, lies, manipulation and disconnect — over time peeled that away.

As the dust settles on the fallout of our done Marriage, I reflect. I'm not bitter, I don't hate you. I do know you now though, your lies can't affect me any more. I was hoping my task in your life was to help you grow to a more pure person, and you would grow through enlightenment and understanding of all your wrongs. That you would want to clear the negative and be honest, admit your wrongs. This though was not what you could do and was not what you have chosen to do. I'm letting you know that my contract is done, my soul contract to you is finished.

My Children are now my focus and they are my death till we part. There really is no need for you to punish me any longer, I have not done anything bad by you. I think it is time for you to stop the dislike towards me and your need to feel you have a control over me. Wanting me to have nothing and to struggle is not fair. Yes, I did finally say no more to you, no more abuse (that is what it was, abuse). I don't need to worry any more, I don't need to constantly stress about how I could make you love me or love us enough. There was no way I could have anyway because you didn't want that life. You wanted to be unfaithful and be your own person doing what Ant wanted all the time. You never understood how to love someone wholly. It's okay and this is the path. However, I now deserve to be really happy, to be me. I hope you can find a peace within you Ant, not everything is about the chase of the next dollar and not everyone is out to destroy you. You have lost a lot in this life and revenge has not served you well. Toxic people are drawn to Toxic situations, stop hanging around toxic people. Find true friends, real people. Not ones that pretend to be.

There is nothing more you can take from me. So be peaceful now and stop plotting your next way to get back at me. Let me be the best I can be to raise the kids, let me be happy, safe, well and strong to raise good, happy and healthy humans. You trying to hurt or hinder me just makes it more difficult for me to do that. Taking my energy away from them. I won't have my kids fall into the cycle of negative pasts turning them into shit humans. It has to stop here.

They are our only link now, but you need to be a positive influence in their life, not an aggressive, confusing person. Don't be the person that speaks badly about the one person that they trust the most: me. Please be a parent to them, not a badly behaved friend, they are not your mates. The kids aren't fully aware of the extent of your manipulation and how you can make them think that the way you talk and act is okay. They love you but can't say why. Because you're their dad and you buy them things. Teach them your wrongs, be truthful and say how those wrongs have impacted you today. Try and break the bullshit cycle your family have of not speaking about problems, because its hard and could be embarrassing. Openness is the key to a healthy relationship, family and soul.

I needed to write this to you as part of my own healing process. It's my way of releasing my soul from yours. The completion of our soul Contract.

Peace to you and your Family. You are free of me.

Thanks x Nikki

ACKNOWLEDGEMENTS

So many people have shaped me into me. I want to thank them.

DAD, my hero. You saved me and taught me so much. **MUM**, you're in that too. Thanks for always being there to listen and raise me up. Now let's get the farm sold — the North awaits you both.

My brother **Leon**, love you. Always calm. Such a good human and creating beautiful humans on your farm.

My sister **Summa**, keep on keepin... you got this, sister. Thank you for encouraging me to move and help me settle in. **Craig** you also get an honourable mention, thank you for helping us, thanks for being a great uncle to the kids.

Nanna, you are my greatest role model. Thank you for everything you did for me. Thank you for the caramel slice. Always telling me to keep dancing.

Pop, love you and miss you. Thank you for watching over me from the other side I know it's you.

Jane, for growing up with me and being with me all the way. The Jane of younger days I will hold close. Wish I didn't know what I do now though, such betrayal.

Sandy, no words but so much love for you and thank you. I would be a lesbian for you. So happy you are settled and a baby is on the way. I know your journey has been long also.

Nicole, love you, thank you for finding me. Without you, I would have not made it. My soul sister.

Emma and the girls (Simone, Anne-Marie, Amanda), thanks for the breaks in the weather. Not so much Simone now as we know why! My main girls in the Wollondilly thanks for the push to get me out of there.

GG- Thanks for the baked dinners when I would come home to visit.

Cherry, thank you for keeping me on track and helping me always. So glad you signed up to dance with me. Whatever the reason you decided I wasn't your person anymore that's okay and I understand. Still love you.

Daniel W, thank you for being my first love and the intensity that went along with it.

The Stuut, Thanks for all your support in everything I do. My creative saviour, my BBQ head man, my chook pen creator and Garden establisher. Thank you for always being at the ready. You may have started out as Ant's friend but I will always call you my friend more lol!

Jed, thank you for writing me poetry all those years ago, making me feel like I was special to someone.

Tania, thank you for being a great boss and an amazing mentor.

Antonio, my husband and my lesson in this life's path, thank you for doing this life with me. Thank you for our children. Even though the pain of this journey with you has been deep I hold no hate to you and hope you find a peace within you soon.

My kids. **Andrew**, for being the best big brother and my main man at home. **Tristan**, thank you for teaching me patience and how to do proper hugs. **Leo,** thank you for really showing me that I need more patience and that loudness is really cool. **Marly,** my baby girl thanks for all your help with the cleaning, thanks for loving dance and knowing how to melt your brothers and soften your father.

My animals – thanks for standing there and listening when I talk.

My entire family and anyone who has lent me money to get by, to feed the kids or pay my rent forever grateful, you're on my IOU list and you will be paid back.

Diana – she won't read this as she is currently living in a Psychiatric ward on the Gold Coast and has no idea what day it even is. I thank her for birthing me and giving me my siblings. My memory of her fades more as the years go on and too much other trauma has happened in my life that my childhood seems too far gone to worry about it now or how it has affected me.

Lastly, I want to thank all the people on the way, all the ones that have come on my life's path, even if it was fleeting. Even those that hurt me greatly or presented me with challenges. You all have taught me a lot and shaped me into who I am today. Without all the encounters I could not be me.

Keep Dancing.

www.ingramcontent.com/pod-product-compliance
Lightning Source LLC
Chambersburg PA
CBHW041317110526
44591CB00021B/2818